DATE DUE

ACTIVITIES FOR CREATING

Pictures & Poetry

Janis Bunchman

and Stephanie Bissell Briggs

Davis Publications, Inc.
Worcester, Massachusetts

This book is dedicated to our families, friends and fellow teachers who share our passion for the arts.

We would like to thank our families for their support and encouragement throughout this project. Without their patience, consideration and time this project could not have been completed. We acknowledge the Lesley College Master's program entitled "Creative Arts in Learning"; our idea for *Pictures & Poetry* was created because of this program. We thank the Summit County School District in Colorado, its teachers, parents and students for their continued support of the arts. We also thank Bonnie and Mike Huffer for the graphic design of our manuscript proposal.

We are happy to share art from the following students attending Summit County Schools: Josh Wessinger, Tawni Mazzone, Jessica Thayer, Abby Paffrath, Cameron Abernathy, Alex Headly, Cari Lewis and Katie Mallouk. We thank Cathy Weisman Topal for the student work created by Ann Runquist, and Binney & Smith's 1992–93 Crayola® Dream-Makers™ program for the work by Emily Erb. We also thank Sarah Zook, who created the artwork on our cover.

Many museums, collectors and publishing companies have been most helpful in obtaining images, portraits and poetry. We thank the following individuals, museums and galleries: David E. White; McDougal, Littel & Company; Studio One Photography; The Bettmann Archive; Mrs. John Hay Whitney; Faith Ringgold; the Museum of Modern Art; Smith College Museum of Art; the Solomon R. Guggenheim Museum; the Amon Carter Museum; the Newark Museum; the Frank Lloyd Wright Foundation; Bertha and Mitchel Siegel; the Metropolitan Museum of Art; the Hyde Collection; Hampton University Museum; the Denver Museum of Natural History; the U.S. Dept. of the Interior, Indian Arts and Crafts Board; the National Gallery, London; and the Albertina Museum, Vienna.

Our appreciation is also extended to these publishers and individuals: Wendell Berry for his poem "Sowing the Seed"; "The Courier-Journal," Louisville, Kentucky for Wendell Berry's photograph; Hancock House Publishers, Ltd. for "My Heart Soars" by Chief Dan George; Harper and Row Publishers, Inc. for "I Paint What I See" by E. B. White; Harcourt Brace Jovanovich, Inc. for "Jazz Fantasia" by Carl Sandburg; Indiana University Press and Mary Ellen Solt for her poem "Forsythia"; Lilian Moore and Marian Reiner for "Outside" by Lilian Moore; Liveright Publishing Corp. for "D-re-A-mi-N-gl-Y" by e. e. cummings; New Directions Publishing for "The Red Wheelbarrow" by William Carlos Williams; and Random House, Inc. for "Dreams" by Langston Hughes.

Finally, we would like to thank our editor Martha Siegel for her faith in this project and her guidance during the process; Nancy Burnett; Wyatt Wade; and Holly Hanson at Davis Publications, Inc. for their time, commitment and support of this project.

Copyright 1994
Davis Publications, Inc.
Worcester, MA U.S.A.

Editor: Martha Siegel
Production Editor: Nancy Burnett
Design: Susan Marsh

Printed in U.S.A.

Library of Congress Catalog Card Number:
93- 72681
ISBN 87192–273–8
10 9 8 7 6 5 4 3

CONTENTS

You are about to begin a fantastic voyage. By traveling back in time — perhaps centuries or maybe only a few years — you will begin to explore the lives of some very creative people. Join the *Pictures & Poetry* adventure as we learn about artists, poets and the works they have each produced, from paintings to folk ballads, sculptures to lyric poems.

On this journey you will learn about the ideas and images that inspire both artists and poets to create. You will learn about the relationship between art and poetry, and will begin to form connections between the two. Along the way you will also learn about exotic places throughout the world — some as far away as Japan, others as close as New York City.

As you read stories about the lives of the fourteen artists and fourteen poets included in *Pictures & Poetry*, you will learn about the unusual times in which they lived. By looking at the artwork and poetry that these people have created, you will begin to understand the creative process — what influences individuals to create and how these influences are expressed. By trying your hand at the activities included in each chapter, you will experience the techniques used by both artists and poets in developing their work. By exploring *Pictures & Poetry*, you will discover something about yourself, as you create artwork and poetry which tells a story about you.

The Structure

The fourteen chapters in *Pictures & Poetry* are filled with a variety of information. Each chapter focuses on the lives and works of an artist and a poet, with lively biographies of each. You will explore original artwork and poetry created by these well-known individuals as they are reproduced in each chapter. Then you will have the opportunity to try out the same techniques and processes used by these

individuals in art and writing activities designed just for you. Finally, each chapter includes a section called "Making the Connection." These sections will guide you through the questions and ideas surrounding the link between the two creative individuals, and a glossary at the back of the book will help you understand the concepts explored here.

Extending the Learning Process

There are many ways to extend the ideas presented in *Pictures & Poetry*. Don't limit your exploration of art and poetry to the activities in each chapter. Go further. Dig deeper. Learn as much as you can, and enjoy yourself.

Activities

Part of the purpose of this book is to help you focus on the *process* of creating both artwork and poetry. While you may end up with a *product* — a poem or an artwork — that is not the primary goal.

To learn the most about the process of creating, try focusing on the basic concepts covered in each art and poetry activity. These "basics" are the building blocks for learning. Start small. Don't try to compose a complete poem right off the bat. Instead, try playing with the sounds and rhythms of your language first. Experiment with lines and brush strokes before attempting a complete painting. Pinch and squeeze your ball of clay before trying to work on a sculpture. These warm-up exercises will help you to become familiar with the building blocks of each concept.

Once you have completed a poem or a work of art, put it aside for a while. Later, come back to your work. Is there anything you want to change now? Try reworking and rewriting. See what can be improved. Start over if you like. Take a fresh look.

The activities we have provided are certainly not the only ways to approach learning about the artists and poets covered. Try extending the activities by acting out the images you see or read in each work. Take different poses. Try out the roles of the different characters in the artwork or poem. Try recording the sounds you "hear" in the works by using a tape cassette recorder. Can you imagine how a painting or sculpture sounds? Can you create these sounds using your voice, hands or body?

Keep an art and poetry journal. Record your thoughts about the work in your journal or about the ideas you have for work of your own. Try using words and drawings to express these ideas. A journal is a good place for private notes, so don't be afraid to write down even the silliest ideas.

Digging deeper

There is a lot to learn about both artists and poets. Try doing you own research to learn more about the creative people in this book. Go to the library. Find other work by them. Learn about how they created other poems and artwork, and how their styles may have changed over time. You might even come across new artists and poets along the way. Try comparing their work with that of the individuals in this book. How is it different? How is it similar?

While you are learning about the connections between art and poetry, you will probably start making connections to other subjects also. Explore these connections. How can you learn about science while studying the artwork of Georgia O'Keeffe? Try planting some flower seeds and learn about how they grow. How can you learn about math when you are studying Wassily Kandisky's paintings? Focus on geometric shapes and learn about how they are constructed.

You might want to learn more about the country or region of an artist or poet. Look at a world map to learn where he or she lived long ago or where they live today. Try playing the music of that area and time period. You might find that listening to this music will inspire you to create your own work, while it also helps you to understand the world of the artist and poet you are exploring. Have a food festival. Explore the cuisine of the featured artist or poet's land. Try cooking up a storm.

Working together

Once you start exploring *Pictures & Poetry*, you will probably want to share your ideas with friends. You might find that you have similar ideas about some of the artwork and poetry in this book. You might have very different ideas. Either way, talk it over. Share your poetry and your art. Offer helpful suggestions about how each person's work could be improved. Learn from each other.

It's for real

You can learn a lot about art from the pictures in this book. You can learn even more by visiting the original artwork in a museum. It is exciting to see the real blobs and brushstrokes of paint on the surface of an artist's canvas. It is thrilling to experience the size and shape of a sculpture, whether it is huge or quite small. If you can, try visiting a local art museum or gallery to experience the feeling of seeing original art.

Now you are ready to start your *Pictures & Poetry* journey. It will be a fantastic voyage. Along the way, we hope you will begin to understand something about how artists and poets create, and that you will learn to appreciate and enjoy this wonderful creative process. Let's begin.

1

Henri Matisse

1859–1954 ✳ FRENCH

Henri Matisse grew up in a small town in northern France. His father earned a living as a grain merchant while his mother painted decorations on fine china. Many days Henri would sit with his mother at the kitchen table and study the fine designs and patterns she painted. Sometimes she would let him paint some of his own designs on old pieces of china.

Matisse's father wanted his son to become a lawyer, so Henri was sent to law school. After receiving his diploma, Matisse returned home to work as a law clerk. But he did not enjoy the work. An appendix operation changed his life. To amuse him while he recovered, his mother bought her son a box of paints, paintbrushes and a do-it-yourself handbook on painting. Matisse discovered a passion for art. Soon he was spending his spare time creating drawings and paintings. He began taking art classes at night and finally left his law job to attend art school.

Matisse's paintings are filled with the bright colors and patterns he loved. When painting indoor scenes, he surrounded his subjects with brightly patterned wall coverings, fabrics, curtains and rugs. The background was often just as important to him as the portrait of a woman or still life of fruit and flowers he was painting. When painting the outdoors, Matisse simplified the shapes of nature to create colorful designs. Many of his paintings of inside spaces include windows that look out on landscapes of gardens, the countryside, oceans, hills and mountains. Rooms filled with richly decorated furniture and lined with patterned wallpaper open up to outdoor scenes that are equally colorful and carefully designed. It is as if Matisse wanted to turn the whole world into a decorative design.

Matisse's art shocked the world when it was first created. People called Matisse and a group of younger painters who followed his style *fauves*, or "wild beasts," for their simplified drawings and use of bright colors. But Matisse said he simply wanted to create "an art which will calm and soothe" people of all professions and from all walks of life.

Window on the World

Window paintings allow an artist to show two different scenes in a single painting. There is an inside and an outside environment, of which both are important. In Matisse's window paintings, the artist made vivid patterns using bold patches of color and repeating lines and shapes on wallpaper, floors and even in the outdoors

You will need

newspaper or other material for
    covering tabletop
painting paper
tempera or watercolor paint
paintbrushes
water cups for rinsing

Henri Matisse.
Photograph:
The Bettmann Archive.

To begin

Doing a window painting is a great way to explore pattern and the environment. Cover your tabletop with newspaper or other protective material. Decide which direction is best for your paper, vertical or horizontal. Draw a window shape somewhere on the sheet of paper, not necessarily in the center. To follow Matisse's approach, you might want to set up a still life in front of a window. Look past the still-life arrangement to the outdoor landscape. Make the landscape either the background of your painting or the most important part, the focus. Find a comfortable place to sit in front of the window. Use the window frame on your paper to paint what you see outside.

Fill the rest of your paper with a pattern that you design. Use only three colors and shapes, and repeat them in various ways. You might choose to use bright colors, as Matisse did. Include furniture and wallpaper as part of the design, or paint a decorative pattern of your own that covers the entire page.

Open Window, 1905. Oil on canvas, 21¾ x 18⅛" (55 x 46 cm). Collection of Mrs. John Hay Whitney.

Josh Wessinger,

OUTSIDE

I
am inside
looking outside
at the pelting
rain —
where
the outside world
is melting
upon my
window
pane.

By Lilian Moore

Lilian Moore

1909– ✳ AMERICAN

When Lilian Moore was a child, she loved to tell stories. She would spend hours telling tales to her friends, each with a suspenseful ending. She also loved to read and would bring home all the books she could carry from the library, reading them as she walked. This was the beginning of her life as a writer.

In college Moore began to enjoy poetry, especially works by the romantic poets John Keats, William Blake and Percy Bysshe Shelley. Later in life she discovered contemporary poets who inspired her to compose her own poetry. She began writing poems drawing on her own childhood experiences and her interests in chamber music, biking, ice skating, reading, gardening and travel.

Moore has worked especially hard to share her love for reading, her stories and poetry with children. She has taught children with special needs how to read, in the belief that children who read develop creative minds that lead them to write stories of their own. In particular, she feels that poetry should be an everyday experience for children, helping them learn how to describe their observations and express their feelings.

In her poem "Outside," Moore writes about her own quiet observation of a rainy day experience. Her description is an example of how a simple event can be expressed in an extraordinary manner.

Lilian Moore.
Courtesy of the artist.
Photograph by Glenn Weston.

Window Worlds

Have you ever looked through a window when it is raining? Lilian Moore has and her poem "Outside" describes this experience. What kinds of patterns have you seen the rain make against your windowpane? Do snow, sunshine and shadows make patterns too? How would you describe these patterns?

Sometimes words can be arranged to make patterns. Look at the words used in "Outside." Notice how they are arranged on different lines. Each line is a special length with a different number of words. The lines are shorter at the top and spread out toward the middle, like two raindrops dripping down a windowpane.

To begin

Take a look outside your window. What sort of things do you see? Is there grass and flowers or buildings and roads? Is the sun shining or is it cloudy and gray? Select one interesting object that you see outside, such as a tree, house or tall building. Make a list of several words or phrases that describe what you see. Try using words that will help the reader of your poem see the view out your window. Your list might look something like this:

tall skyscrapers
sturdy
rising
climbing like a vine

Place your words and phrases on different lines. Try to arrange them so that they give an illusion of the subject outside your window, just as the words in Lilian Moore's poem looked like raindrops. Can you describe your window observation in a poetry pattern?

MAKING THE CONNECTION

When you look through a window, you might see clouds, rain, trees and rivers. Your window might not hold a view of nature, but instead a brick wall, a crowded street or electrical wires. Whatever the actual view, the poet and artist can transform what they see into images worth painting or writing about. Both Matisse and Moore used their imaginations to create windows through which their audiences can view nature in simple yet vivid forms. Matisse, often painting from memory or depicting places he had only read about, created windows that communicated the serene, detached way he viewed the world. Moore used poetry to express her love for and keen awareness of nature, and to help readers relate to everyday experiences they have seen or imagined. These artists used their words and pictures to open windows for others to heighten their perceptions of the world around them.

The Building

The
tall
sturdy
skyscraper
rising
high
climbs
like
a
vine
to
the
sky
above.

First grade class poem

2

Faith Ringgold

1930– ✳ AFRICAN AMERICAN

The most important artistic influence on Faith Ringgold was her mother. As a little girl, Faith was often sick with asthma, and she spent many hours at home. Her mother, a fashion designer and dressmaker, often sat with her daughter while she worked, giving the child pieces of material to entertain herself with. When Faith went off to college and graduate school to study painting, she was not aware of the importance of her mother's early influence. At school she learned how to draw and paint and about the art and artists of Europe. But she did not learn anything about how to express herself as an African-American woman. After leaving school, Ringgold began to teach herself. She remembered the beautiful fabrics and clothing her mother created and designed. She began studying African art. At the same time, she became involved in the civil rights movement in the United States and grew especially concerned about the rights of African-American women. Her art began to reflect these concerns.

With the help of her mother, Ringgold began creating portrait masks and doll-like soft sculptures of women she knew in Harlem and New York and of famous African Americans like Martin Luther King, Jr. She had learned that these types of crafts were common in Africa. Patterned fabric, beads, fringe and embroidery were used for the faces and costumes of her characters. Often she created the females with their mouths open to show the need for African-American women to speak out for their rights. To tell the experience of African Americans in America, she began performing with her soft sculptures and masks.

Ringgold also began making quilts, sometimes working together with her mother, piecing together fabric squares onto which she paints or attaches soft sculptures. She also writes stories about the lives of black women, which she paints on the quilts. Ringgold believes quilting is a powerful way to tell about women's lives because women have been expressing themselves as quiltmakers for generations.

More recently Ringgold has begun writing and illustrating books for children. In these stories, she is able to bring her love for storytelling together with her love for art.

Personality Soft Sculptures

A soft sculpture can be made to look like someone you know, a character in a book or an image you have seen. The life-size soft sculptures of Faith Ringgold sometimes tell a person's story or resemble a personality of the past.

You will need

12 x 18" drawing paper
pencil
sharp scissors
scrap pieces of felt and other fabrics
pins
sewing needle and thread
polyester fiberfill
buttons, yarn, beads and shells
craft or fabric glue or a hot glue gun

Faith Ringgold, 1989.
Courtesy of the artist.
Photograph by Lucille Tortora.

To begin

Think of a person or character you would like to use as a model for a soft personality sculpture. What will your sculpture represent and what kind of story will you tell about it?

Soft sculptures can be made of almost any scraps of fabric and soft material you can find. On a piece of 12 x 18" paper, draw a simple outline of the figure to use as a pattern. The figure could be someone in action, such as playing basketball or dancing. Lay the pattern on the material you have chosen, pin the pattern in place, and cut out the pieces. The sculpture could be constructed of a single doll shape, in which the head, arms, trunk and legs are cut in one continuous piece. Another approach would be to cut the head and body as one shape and add on material for the arms and legs. The arms and legs could be in the same pattern or done separately. Stitch around the outside edges of your pieces, remembering to leave an opening for the stuffing. Use polyester fiberfill to stuff all the parts of the sculpture and sew the parts together.

Mrs. Jones and Family, 1973. Sewn fabric and embroidery, 60 x 12 x 16" (152 x 30 x 41 cm). Courtesy of the artist. Photograph by Karen Bell.

Give the face the personality you are depicting by adding materials like buttons, yarn, beads and shells for the eyes, nose, mouth and hair. These can be attached with craft or fabric glue. Fur, feathers, shells, twigs and other natural materials can be used for the clothes and decorations on the sculptures. The figures can be freestanding or hung on a wall.

Tawni Mazzone, grade 5.

WE WEAR THE MASK

We wear the mask that grins and lies,
It hides our cheeks and shades our eyes, —
This debt we pay to human guile;
With torn and bleeding hearts we smile,
And mouth with myriad subtleties.
Why should the world be otherwise,
In counting all our tears and sighs?
Nay, let them only see us, while
   We wear the mask.

We smile, but, O great Christ, our cries
To thee from tortured souls arise.
We sing, but oh the clay is vile
Beneath our feet, and long the mile;
But let the world dream otherwise,
   We wear the mask!

By Paul Laurence Dunbar

Paul Laurence Dunbar.
Photograph: The Bettmann Archive.

Paul Laurence Dunbar

1872–1906 ✳ AFRICAN AMERICAN

The son of freed slaves, Paul Laurence Dunbar grew up to protest racial discrimination in his essays, stories and poetry. Paul's father escaped slavery by fleeing to Canada along the Underground Railroad and came back to serve in the Union Army during the Civil War. His mother was freed at the end of the War and settled in Ohio, where she met Paul's father.

Dunbar was always close to his mother. He first became fascinated with language as a child while listening to her tell stories. He became intrigued with words, especially rhyme, and began to recite in church the poetry he had written in school. His mother hoped that one day he would be a preacher, but Dunbar knew he would become a writer.

Dunbar was one of only a few African Americans in his high school. He did not remember feeling the effects of racial discrimination during those years, when he wrote poetry and funny anecdotes for the school paper. He was an active debater and a member of the school's literary society. One of his poems was selected as the class song. Dunbar was also friends with Orville and Wilbur Wright. Few people know that before the Wright brothers took their historic flight at Kitty Hawk, they had a printing business. They printed the early editions of an experimental newspaper Dunbar created for African-American readers, the first such newspaper in Dayton, Ohio.

After high school Dunbar had trouble getting a job because he was black. He finally found a job running an elevator. In his spare time, he continued to write poems and stories for newspapers. He also wrote essays protesting injustices against African Americans. Eventually his work was published, and Dunbar began to gain some fame. His plantation tales and adventure stories of black life in American cities became known for portraying African-American life realistically. Many of his stories and poems, such as "We Wear the Mask," deal with the pain of racial discrimination.

Imaginary Masks

Have you ever wished you could be some-one else for a day? Maybe you've thought about becoming a character from a book you're reading, the president of the United States or even an animal! When you wear a mask, you can be any charac-ter you imagine. Paul Laurence Dunbar wrote about wearing a mask of smiles to hide behind pain and tears. He may have been referring to the pain of racial dis-crimination, which made him feel he had to hide behind a false smile, pretending he was not hurt.

To begin

Put on an imaginary mask (or a real one if you have it) and write a poem about the new you. Begin by asking yourself questions about how it feels to hide behind your mask. Try to answer these questions without using any of the words in the original questions. Try using a single, repeated phase in your answers. Repetition is found in many poems. In "We Wear the Mask," it begins in the first sentence, and occurs again at the end of each following paragraph. Think of a line you can repeat which will help emphasize the point of your poem.

MAKING THE CONNECTION

A symbol is something that stands for or represents another thing. The mask can be a symbol to cover up feelings, to show emotions or to represent a person or animal. Both Dunbar and Ringgold used the face or mask as a symbol of identity. When Dunbar wrote his poetry during the 1800s, he used symbols to relate to the life of an African American in the United States at the turn of the century. In "We Wear the Mask," the mask is a symbol of a time of charade, when Dunbar felt that African Americans often believed they had to hide their anger and pain over discrimination behind smiling faces. Ringgold uses the symbolism of masks and faces to tell the story of her heritage, in which African-American women have often had to hide their needs and emotions from a hostile world. Both artists felt a need to tell of the struggles in the lives of their own families and those of generations past, struggles that were frequently concealed from outsiders.

Poets and artists also use masks to offer people a way to get outside of themselves and sample another person's view of the world. We can be reminded of the struggles in past generations, be made aware of present lives or gain insight about what might be in the future.

The Mask of a Lion

How do you feel? I am proud and strong.
Why do you feel that way? All other animals are frightened of me.
(Repetitive line) I fear nothing.

Where do you live? The jungle is my home.
What is it like there? The earth is green and alive.
(Repetitive line) I fear nothing.

What do you like to do? Resting in the warm sun makes me content.
Why do you enjoy this activity? It is a peaceful time.
(Repetitive line) I fear nothing.

What is your dream? I wish to freely roam the earth.
What do you ask of mankind? Keep your weapons down.
(Repetitive line, this time with a message) So — I can fear nothing.

By John Martin, grade 3

3

Alexander Calder

1898–1976 ✳ AMERICAN

Alexander Calder, called Sandy by his friends, had a keen imagination and sense of humor, which he used freely in his work. He was born into a family of artists; his grandfather and father were sculptors and his mother was a painter. As a youth, Calder preferred working with tools, and he studied to become an engineer. It was not until Calder was an adult that he discovered his interest in art. Inspired by his love for mechanical toys, he began creating surprising and innovative sculptures that continue to delight people of all ages.

Calder first created toys and figures to amuse himself and his friends. One such work is his mechanical recreation of the circus. He loved the circus and would go to see it over and over again, observing each act and detail of the performers. Out of bits of wire, corks and spools, he created his own circus complete with trapeze artists, acrobats, clowns, trained dogs, animal cages and crowds of people. All of the figures could move, and Calder would hold performances in the evenings under a big top and spotlight, astounding audiences at how realistic his wire performers appeared.

Calder continued to experiment with sculpture and became best known for his invention of *mobiles,* hanging sculptures with parts that move. He used wires to support metal discs cut into geometric or irregular, free-form shapes painted in his favorite colors of red, blue, yellow, black and green. At first Calder made his mobiles move mechanically, with little motors or hand cranks. Later he refined them to wave and spin with the natural currents of the air around them.

Calder's love for nature can be seen in the forms and patterns of movement in his mobiles. Although the forms are often abstract, they suggest objects and rhythms in nature, like fish in the sea, wind in the trees or the flow of tides. In his *Lobster Trap and Fish Tail* mobile, for example, the torpedo-like shape at the top of the mobile suggests the body of a lobster, while the delicate wire cage looks like a trap. The repeated triangular shapes below could be a school of fish. Constructed of wire and painted aluminum, the mobile stretches fifteen feet wide, but it is so light and delicate that its motion in the air mimics the fluid movements of creatures under the sea.

Alexander Calder, 1973.
Photograph: UPI/Bettmann.

Art in Motion

Mobiles are sculptures with attached, movable parts that hang from a single point and rotate with changes in the wind or air currents. They must be balanced in a way that allows part to hang straight. When correctly balanced, mobiles can move freely, producing a variety of color and shadow patterns.

You will need

sticks, coat hangers, wooden dowels or
   heavy cardboard
white glue
string or light-gauge wire
variety of cardboard shapes (different
   colors, if available, or painted)
small pieces of wood, Styrofoam or plastic
paint or felt-tipped markers
paintbrushes
water cups for rinsing
hole puncher
thread or yarn

To begin

A mobile can be created from a variety of materials. It is best to begin with the hanging or supporting arm of the mobile, to which all other pieces are connected. It can be designed in a cross pattern or a hanger form, so many objects can hang from it. You can use sticks, coat hangers, wooden dowels or heavy cardboard to form the arm. If you use dowels or sticks in a cross pattern, be sure to connect the two pieces of wood securely. First apply glue to the sticks, then use wire or string to bind the sticks together. Let the glue dry before hanging pieces from the sticks.

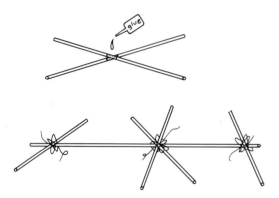

Next decide which items you want to hang from your mobile arm structure. Balance is the essential principle. Each part of the mobile must be balanced using small objects and larger objects together so that no one side outweighs any other, causing the mobile to tilt. You may want to choose a theme for your structure, such as free-form shapes or shapes in nature (fish, flowers, leaves). Decide on the number of shapes to be used in the mobile. Use cardboard, wood, Styrofoam or plastic to create shapes that fit your theme. Think about which colors you will use and how the colors and sizes of shapes will work together in your mobile. Use paints or felt-tipped markers to decorate each piece.

Use a hole puncher to make a hole in the top of each shape. This will be the hole

Lobster Trap and Fish Tail, 1939. Hanging mobile: painted steel wire and sheet aluminum, about 8' 6" high x 9' 6" diameter (2.60 x 2.90 m).
The Museum of Modern Art, New York. Commissioned by the Advisory Committee for the stairwell of the Museum.

Fourth grade group project.

from which each shape will hang from your mobile. Attach a thread, wire or string through the hole in each object, tying it securely. Attach the other end of the threads to the support arm. The thread, wire or yarn might need to be cut to different lengths so the objects hang evenly, and the threads might have to be moved around on the support arm to balance the hanging mobile.

Making mobiles involves a lot of experimentation to see what shapes balance and look pleasing for the sculptural form. You might need to try many different ways before you decide on the mobile that is balanced and in the form you like.

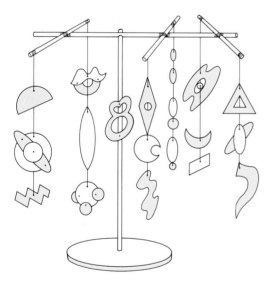

Variation

The stabile is a variation of the hanging mobile. It is mounted on a platform so that it stands up and is self-supporting. Constructing a stabile is another way for you to explore the sculpture of Alexander Calder.

William Carlos Williams

1883–1963 ✳ AMERICAN

William Carlos Williams had an unusual career: he was both a doctor *and* a poet. He started writing poetry after he began studying medicine, and he believed that his medical training helped his poetry. "The scientist is very important to the poet, because his language is important to him," Williams said. He felt that precise language should be used in both professions.

Williams belonged to a group of writers and artists who were interested in experimenting with art. They met at different locations to share ideas and critique each others' work. These meetings influenced Williams's writing. He began writing short poems using simple language to describe the things that made up his life in his home state of New Jersey. His poems describe common, everyday objects and scenes with the precision of a scientist while at the same time expressing the beauty he saw in them as a poet.

"The Red Wheelbarrow" is one of Williams's best-known works. Here the poet shows how he sees a humble, everyday scene in a new way. Although the poem is very short, the breaks in the lines and long vowel sounds in the words slow reading down. The motion of reading this poem slowly is like the long look Williams is taking at the red

wheelbarrow and the white chickens after the rain. It is as if he is seeing the beauty in these simple objects for the first time. The wonder expressed in the rhythm of the words shows us that even the simplest things in life have value and importance.

William Carlos Williams, 1958. Photograph: UPI/Bettmann Newsphotos.

THE RED WHEELBARROW

so much depends
upon

a red wheel
barrow

glazed with rain
water

beside the white
chickens

By William Carlos Williams

Words in Motion

Simple objects in everyday settings — such as a wheelbarrow in a farmyard — can become the inspiration for simple yet dynamic poetry. In observing and recording impressions of the environment, poets help us to recognize the beauty in even the most common objects. Are there everyday objects in your school or home which you could observe closely and then describe with great simplicity? In "The Red Wheelbarrow," William Carlos Williams describes his environment and helps us to notice the unusual qualities of a wheelbarrow: its simple form when at rest, and its potential for movement along the rocky and rain-splashed paths of a farmyard.

MAKING THE CONNECTION

A wheelbarrow and a mobile are both created with movement in mind, and both depend on balance to operate successfully. As it moves about in the air, a mobile has the potential for presenting an onlooker with many different views. In a similar way, the word picture of a wheelbarrow resting in the rain might bring to mind potential movements of the tool in use. Balance in a mobile is achieved by the weighing, sizing and placement of parts. In a poem, balance is created by the choices and placement of words. In poetry *imagery* is a way of using language to make an object seem so real that a reader can almost experience it. In "The Red Wheelbarrow," Williams uses color and a sense of touch to make the wheelbarrow a vision you could almost feel. Calder used imagery to suggest motion. He would study a simple object such as a wheelbarrow along with items that might go in it, then play with the parts to make a balanced moving sculpture. Many of his mobiles of fish and birds give a feeling of rolling motion.

To begin

Take a walk and make a list of some of the simple objects you see. Look for items that have either rhythm, balance or movement. Select one object to write a free-verse poem about. Don't worry about any specific rules of length, rhyme or meter. Simply convey observations, thoughts, feelings and words in a meaningful way. You may want your poem to be short, clear and precise with one to three words on each line like Williams's poem. Think carefully about where to place each word. Share how the object looks in your mental picture.

Stars

The stars
above

the rising
buildings

buzz
by the yellow
moon

*Second grade
class poem*

4

Diego Rivera

1886–1957 ✳ MEXICAN

Diego Rivera loved to draw and paint. As a little boy, he would entertain people by painting pictures of family and friends. His father even set up a room in his house where Diego could use entire walls to paint. It is probably no surprise, then, that Rivera grew up to become an artist who communicated his ideas in a big way.

After attending art school in Mexico and Europe, Rivera became famous for painting large murals in the cities of Mexico. He painted murals on the sides of buildings and on brick walls. He also created mosaic murals, huge pictures formed by gluing together pieces of small, colored clay tiles or colored bits of glass.

Rivera's murals tell stories of the Mexican people and their struggles for an easier life. They show the marketplace, working people, parents and children and the surrounding landscape of Mexico. Many of his murals picture events from the Mexican revolution of 1910, when the Mexican people fought for the right to control their own lives. Rivera's murals caused controversy in some places, but most people liked the way he told the history of the Mexican people. Even today these murals, which can be seen on public buildings in Mexico and the United States, are powerful reminders of Mexican history and an inspiration to artists and viewers alike.

Self-Portrait, 1941. Oil on canvas, 23 x 16⅞" (61 x 43 cm). Smith College Museum of Art, Northampton, Massachusetts. Gift of Irene Rich Clifford, 1977.

Mosaic Murals

Wall paintings known as *murals* can be seen on buildings around the world. Artists use walls as a large format for showing a variety of subjects, such as the everyday life of a country or town, landscapes or political issues. Some of these paintings are made in sections by several artists, each contributing a small portion to the larger picture. This is a type of mural known as a mosaic, in which small parts of the image are pieced together to form the whole work.

You will need

heavyweight cardboard cut into squares
    approximately 6 x 6"
two large sheets of drawing paper
pencil
black felt-tipped marker
scissors
tempera or acrylic paints
paintbrushes
water cups for rinsing
white glue
large piece of butcher paper

To begin

A mural can be a fun group project. Together you can decide on a theme for the mural — like life in your city or town, or the everyday events of cultures from around the world — and each person can contribute a piece to the larger mural design. Lay out blank 6 x 6" pieces of cardboard on a flat working surface. Have the group work together to draw your ideas on a piece of paper big enough for the cardboard squares to fit on. (Eighteen squares can make a 1½ x 3' mural.)

When the main composition has been sketched, divide the surface with pencil and ruler into 6" squares. Trace over the pencil drawing with black felt-tipped marker so the design can be seen easily. Next decide on a color scheme for everyone to follow. Number each square of the drawing and number the backs of corresponding cardboard squares. This will make the mural easy to assemble when finished. Paint the cardboard squares to duplicate the designs on the squares of the drawing paper. Glue completed cardboard squares on a large piece of butcher paper for display on a wall. Make up a title for your mural to give viewers information about your theme.

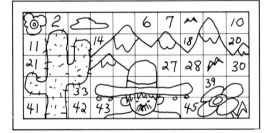

Variation

This activity can also be done with unpainted ceramic tiles. Acrylic paint can be used to add color to each tile. The paint can be sealed with an acrylic medium, and the tiles can be glued together on a wall to form a permanent mural.

People Feed Each Other, panel 9 from the Education Ministry murals, 1923–28. From a slide by Rosenthal Art Slides, Inc., Chicago. Photograph by Mark Rogovin.

Second grade group mural.

E. B. White

1899–1985 ✳ AMERICAN

The writer E. B. White was fond of saying he was born lucky, but he was also born scared. Although his childhood was generally happy, he was afraid of the dark, afraid of the future, afraid of returning to school after the summer. As he grew older, his fears changed but never disappeared. Two things soothed and reassured him all his life. One was the natural world. He often felt closer to animals than to people. The other was writing. When he was only seven or eight years old, White recalled, he looked at a blank sheet of paper and thought, "This is where I belong, this is it."

After graduating from college, White wandered across America and through Europe, always writing. He held a number of temporary jobs as a journalist and was often unemployed. Eventually he was hired by a new literary magazine in New York City, *The New Yorker*. The editors there liked the easygoing, funny tone of White's essays and poems. "I Paint What I See" is one such poem, in which the author humorously champions the cause of artistic freedom. In this ballad he tells the story of how the rich and conservative Nelson Rockefeller objected to Diego Rivera's mural in his New York City building, Rockefeller Center.

White left *The New Yorker* for a time to move with his wife to a farm in Maine. There he worked on essays and poetry and began writing stories for children. White loved writing for children because of the way they could easily make the leap from the real world to make-believe. The first book he wrote for young people was *Stuart Little,* the adventures of a mouse-boy born to human parents. The character appeared to him in a dream and was first written to entertain White's six-year-old niece. His love for animals and farm life was the source of his most famous and best-loved work, *Charlotte's Web.*

I PAINT WHAT I SEE

"What do you paint, when you paint on
    a wall?"
    Said John D.'s grandson Nelson.
"Do you paint just anything there at all?"
"Will there be any doves, or a tree in fall?"
"Or a hunting scene, like an English hall?"

    "I paint what I see," said Rivera.

"What are the colors you use when
    you paint?"
    Said John D.'s grandson Nelson.
"Do you use any red in the beard of a saint?"
"If you do, is it terribly red, or faint?"
"Do you use any blue? Is it Prussian?"

    "I paint what I paint," said Rivera.

"Whose is that head that I see on my wall?"
    Said John D.'s grandson Nelson.
"Is it anyone's head whom we know, at all?"
"A Rensselaer, or a Saltonstall?"
"Is it Franklin D.? Is it Mordaunt Hall?"
"Or is it the head of a Russian?"

    "I paint what I think," said Rivera.

"I paint what I paint, I paint what I see,
"I paint what I think," said Rivera,
"And the thing that is dearest in life to me
"In a bourgeois hall is Integrity;
"However . . .
"I'll take out a couple of people drinkin'
"And put in a picture of Abraham Lincoln;
"I could even give you McCormick's reaper
"And still not make my art much cheaper.
    "But the head of Lenin has got to stay
    "Or my friends will give me the
      bird today,
"The bird, the bird, forever."

E. B. White*, 1954.*
Photograph: UPI/Bettmann Newsphotos.

"It's not good taste in a man like me,"
  Said John D.'s grandson Nelson,
"To question an artist's integrity
"Or mention a practical thing like a fee,
"But I know what I like to a large degree,
  "Though art I hate to hamper;
"For twenty-one thousand conservative
  bucks
"You painted a radical. I say shucks,
  "I never could rent the offices —
  "The capitalistic offices.
"For this, as you know, is a public hall
"And people want doves, or a tree in fall,
"And though your art I dislike to hamper,
"I owe a little to God and Gramper,
  "And after all,
  "It's my wall . . ."

  "We'll see if it is," said Rivera.

By E. B. White

MAKING THE CONNECTION

Freedom of expression with no constraints was important to both White and Rivera, who believed they should be able to write and paint about their thoughts, feelings and observations even if they were controversial. White wrote the poem "I Paint What I See" after Rivera painted a mural on the RCA Building at Rockefeller Center in New York for its owner, Nelson Rockefeller. A staunch capitalist, Rockefeller had ordered Rivera to remove a portrait of Lenin, a Russian revolutionary leader, which was on the artwork. Rivera refused, but offered to include Abraham Lincoln to offset the communist leader. Rockefeller would not agree to Rivera's suggestion, and Rivera would not conform to Rockefeller's demands, so the mural was destroyed. White was so inspired by the stance Rivera took on the mural, which was similar to the way White felt about his own rights and duty as a poet, that he wrote "I Paint What I See."

A Story in Time

"I Paint What I See" is a *ballad. Folk ballads* are among the oldest forms of poetry, often written anonymously. Long ago they were shared mostly orally, and they often changed as different people relayed them. Sometimes the ballads were made into musical selections and sung. Many songs in folk and country music are ballads that tell a story. When the author of a ballad is known, as in "I Paint What I See," it is called a *literary ballad.*

To begin

Ballads are often written in quatrain form, in which a stanza is made up of four lines. There is usually a line that repeats, as in "I Paint What I See." Begin composing your own ballad by writing a story using several quatrains. You might repeat a line at the end of each stanza. Be sure to include action and suspense as you paint your tale with words.

The Ballad of the Bee

The boy stood looking at a tree
Waiting, Watching a bumblebee.
"Please don't sting me was his plea,"
as he knelt on one bent knee.
"Oh no!"
The bee flew down as fast he could
Out the tree made of a hardwood.
He buzzed in front of where the boy stood
What would the result be — bad or good?
"Oh no!"

By Brianna Bissell, grade 6

5

Elizabeth Catlett

1919– ✳ AFRICAN AMERICAN

Elizabeth Catlett's interest in art began when she was a young girl growing up in Washington, D.C. She loved to draw and paint, and her parents encouraged her artistic interests. Her mother provided her with materials, a place to work and time apart. Although her father died when she was young, she was inspired by his accomplishments, as a professor who also played the violin, mandolin and piano, wrote music and carved wood.

Catlett received her art degree from Howard University. She went on to graduate school, where she studied with Grant Wood, a famous American painter. Even though their styles were different, Wood had a significant impact on the direction of Catlett's art. He encouraged her to become a sculptor and to create art about things she knew about from her own experiences. As a result, her work focused increasingly on African-American women and the rights of oppressed people.

Homage to My Young Black Sisters celebrates the efforts of young African-American women fighting for their rights in the civil rights movement of the 1960s. Its abstract style reflects Catlett's awareness of African art and its impact on modern sculpture. She has said about her work, "I have always wanted my art to service my people — to reflect us, to relate to us, to stimulate us, to make us aware of our potential . . . . We have to create an art for liberation and for life."

On a visit to Mexico, Catlett fell in love with that country and its art. She saw a connection between the struggles of the Mexican people as depicted in their murals and the plight of African Americans in the United States. She became a citizen of Mexico, the first women professor at the National School of Fine Arts and eventually the Head of its sculpture department. She now lives and sculpts in Cuernevaca, Mexico..

Elizabeth Catlett.
Photograph by Lillian Gee.

Action Figures

Shape and form are important parts of all three-dimensional objects. Coupled with light, reflections and shadows, these elements can make ordinary forms become dynamic sculptures charged with movement and life. For centuries artists have made images of people in a variety of media and styles either in realistic or abstract forms.

Ballet Dancer, Jessica Thayer, grade 4.

You will need

newspaper or other table covering
oil-based clay
photographs of sculptures that portray
    people in action, or magazine pictures
    of action figures
small tools for sculpting clay
    (pencils, sticks,
    paper clips, etc.)

To begin

Basic geometric forms like cylinders, squares, rectangles and spheres are the building blocks from which a clay sculpture can develop. From these simple forms, you can model dynamic human or animal figure sculptures. A cylinder is the easiest form to begin with. Think about creating a sculpture of a person in action, doing something like playing a sport, dancing or running.

Cover a working surface with newspaper or other protective material. Begin the sculpture with a big clay cylinder (approximately 6" long and 3" thick) for the body of the figure. Use your fingers to squeeze a neck shape, forming an oval or egg shape for the head at the top of the cylinder. Coils the length and width of your finger can be used to form arms and legs. Attach these forms by smoothing one end of each coil to the cylinder form of the body. Once the basic body shape is made, the clay can be easily molded and shaped to make the figure appear to be in action. How will your figure pose? Will the figure be sitting or standing? How can you mold it to make it look like it is running or dancing? Look at photographs of sculptures portraying people in action, or at magazine pictures of action figures. Think about what kind of props you would like to include with your figure. Use extra clay to form a chair, baseball bat, book or whatever forms are appropriate. Details like facial expressions, hair and clothing can be added by using pencils, paper clips and other simple tools to create interesting lines and textures.

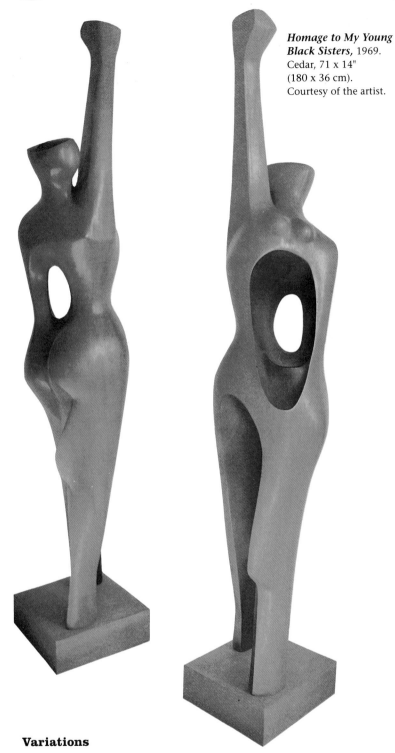

Homage to My Young Black Sisters, 1969. Cedar, 71 x 14" (180 x 36 cm). Courtesy of the artist.

Variations

The oil-based clay can be painted with acrylic paints to add color and details to your sculpture. A clear acrylic medium can be painted on the dry, painted surface to seal the colors and give the oil-based clay the look of a ceramic clay sculpture.

FORSYTHIA

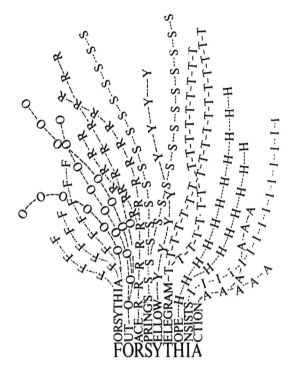

By Mary Ellen Solt

Mary Ellen Solt

1920– ✳ AMERICAN

Mary Ellen Solt is celebrated for her experimental poetry both in the United States and outside the country. She has helped to spread a form of writing called concrete poetry more than any other person. Concrete poetry involves arranging the letters or words that describe an object into a visual image that also describes the object. It is a kind of "painting" with letters or words as the medium.

Solt remembers how she began writing concrete poetry. One day she wanted to write a poem about some yellow crocuses blooming in the snow outside her window. She started thinking of words that began with the letters of *yellow crocus.* For some reason, she began arranging these words in a circle fanning out from the center of the page, turning the paper around and around. When she was done, she realized the picture she had created with words looked more like a rose than a crocus and that the words she had used did not really describe crocuses. She went to work creating a new poem in the same way, entitled "White Rose." To her surprise, the poem was published.

Solt went on to write a whole book of flower poems in which she arranged her words to resemble the way each flower grows. In "Forsythia," she positioned words beginning with the letters of *forsythia* and their Morse code equivalents to create a kind of drawing of a forsythia plant. She placed the poem on a background of bright yellow, the same color as the forsythia flower. Solt still loves creating concrete poems because she believes they make people think carefully about what words really mean and the images they create in our minds.

Poetry Patterns

Concrete poetry is a form of writing that combines letters, words, shapes and ideas to make both mental and visual pictures. The actual shape of a poem's subject is often created by the way the words are arranged. In "Forsythia," poet Mary Ellen Solt fancifully combines Morse code with the words in her poem to "draw" a forsythia flower on the printed page. This makes the words and ideas of a poem as important as the visual image they create on paper.

To begin

Look around you for objects that have interesting forms or occupy space in an unusual manner. Mary Ellen Solt is intrigued by the forms of flowers and the patterns in which they grow. What forms interest you? Make a list of these items, then select one to create a concrete poem. First think about what you want to say or convey about your subject. Are you most interested in the shape of the object, or the way it moves, grows, smells or tastes? Make a list of the words you might use to describe these different characteristics, then play with the words to form a picture. Arrange the words on paper in a manner which conveys your ideas about the object. Think about varying the words you use, the shapes and sizes of letter forms included, and the positioning of these elements on the page.

The Worm

THE WORM WIGGLES AND JIGGLES

By Ian Roberts, Kindergarten

MAKING THE CONNECTION

Catlett's sculpture and Solt's poems are examples of concrete art forms. Each artist takes a subject that has personal meaning and creates a visual representation of it, something other people can appreciate just by looking at it. The shape of Solt's poem and the form of Catlett's sculpture each suggest something about the meaning of the works. Solt's visual representation of a forsythia plant is expressive of the appearance of the plant itself, but also speaks of the plant as a symbol of growth, energy and hope. Notice how she used the first letters of the word *forsythia* to form the words appearing at the bottom of the poem: forsythia, out, races, spring's, yellow, telegram, hope, insists, action. Read as a sentence, these words express the poet's personal viewpoint. Catlett's sculpture suggests the form of two women, fists raised in the air. These forms also suggest something about the artist's viewpoint; her belief in the strength and potential of all African-American women. Both Catlett and Solt use their work to visually express their strong personal ideas.

6

Wassily Kandinsky

1864–1944 ✳ RUSSIAN

Wassily Kandinsky was born in Moscow. As a child, art and music lessons were his favorite activities. Although he grew up to become a lawyer, he never got over the excitement and joy he felt when making music and painting. When he was thirty, he decided to leave Russia and move to Munich, Germany, to study painting seriously.

As an art student, Kandinsky struggled to find a painting style of his own. One day he returned to his studio at twilight. He saw on his easel a painting of what he called "indescribable beauty," even though he could not tell what was painted on the canvas. All he could see were forms and color. Eventually he realized that what he was seeing was his own painting, upside down!

From that time on, Kandinsky created a new kind of painting, called *nonobjective art*. He stopped trying to represent or suggest any recognizable objects and began using lines, whimsical shapes and bright colors to create interesting arrangements in an expressive way.

Kandinsky's interests in painting and music came together in this new art style. He believed that the elements of line and color created a sense of movement and particular moods in his paintings just as musical notes and arrangements do in songs. Kandinsky thought you could "hear" the sound of his paintings if you looked carefully enough. As a result, many of his paintings have musical titles like *harmonies* or *improvisations*.

Wassily Kandinsky, 1912. Courtesy of the Solomon R. Guggenheim Museum.

Rhythm Collage

Some paintings are more complex than others; they may have meanings and associations that are new to us or difficult to understand. The mood of such artworks may be set by the use of colors and the placement of a variety of shapes, without any recognizable objects. Wassily Kandinsky used a brilliant flow of colors and overlapping of various geometric shapes to create balance and movement in his paintings. In a rhythm *collage,* shapes of different sizes and colors can be arranged on a background to produce a similar effect.

You will need

newspaper or other material for
    covering tabletop
variety of pre-cut shapes to use as
    templates for tracing
12 x 18" sheets of paper
pencil
oil pastels
tempera, acrylic or watercolor paints
paintbrushes
water cups for rinsing

To begin

Think about creating a collage with colors and shapes that flow together to give a feeling of *rhythm,* or ordered movement produced by repeating some art element. Cover a tabletop with newspaper or other protective material, and arrange a variety of pre-cut shapes in various patterns on a sheet of 12 x 18" paper. Think of repeated shapes in different sizes as in the repetition of beats and chords in music. Shapes can overlap to suggest objects near or farther away. When your arrangement is complete, trace the shapes lightly with pencil. After the tracing is done, draw over the pencil lines with heavy lines using oil pastels.

Improvisation 28, 1912. Oil on canvas, 43⅞ x 63⅞" (111 x 162 cm). Courtesy of the Solomon R. Guggenheim Museum.

The oil pastel outlines will give distinction to the shapes and help keep the paints used to fill in the shapes from running into each other. You might paint several colors in one shape, creating patterns of solid colors, stripes or designs. The entire picture might be filled with only two colors, showing the various tints and shades that can be achieved when white or black is added. You might want to separate your painting into sections, choosing to paint the spaces with several colors. Playing music while you work can help you feel a sense of rhythm and balance as you arrange the shapes in your picture.

Playground, Ann Runquist, grade 4.

e. e. cummings

1894-1962 ✻ AMERICAN

Edward Estlin Cummings grew up in a remarkable home, with caring, creative parents who encouraged him to develop his imagination and artistic talents. As a little boy, his mother read to him great adventures of literature like *The Jungle Books, Treasure Island, Robinson Crusoe* and *Tom Sawyer*. She also wrote poetry and showed her son how to keep a diary and write stories and poems of his own. Cummings's father was a minister and professor at Harvard University. He also loved to paint and to work with his hands, building additions to the family's summer home or a tree house for his children. From this happy childhood, filled with imaginative play and creative opportunities, e. e. cummings (as he identified himself) went on to spend a lifetime painting and writing poems. When asked if creating paintings and poems interfered with each other, he said "Quite the contrary; they love each other dearly."

His love of painting inspired cummings to create a new style of poetry. In many of his poems, cummings encourages the reader to use the senses of sight and sound to capture a fleeting impression of nature. The printed letters and words are arranged on the page to suggest the movement or look of his subject, like creating a drawing with words. He also tried to capture the sounds of his subjects by breaking up or rearranging words, playing with capital and lowercase letters and shifting around the punctuation of his poems.

"D-re-A-mi-N-gl-Y" is one such poem. It is arranged vertically, possibly to look like the shape of a tree. The first word is stretched out with hyphens and broken up with capital and lowercase letters suggesting the drawn-out and wave-like quality of a dream. The word *(sEe)* is emphasized to encourage the reader to imagine the magical quality of leaves glowing in a sunset, gently blown by the wind. The word *t-ReMbLiN-g* is broken up to mimic the look and motion of the leaves. The little marks of punctuation at the end look like they, too, are trembling. Also, because periods and commas are punctuation marks that ask us to stop while reading a sentence, grouping the marks at the end of the piece encourages readers to pause a moment and savor this vivid little poem.

D-re-A-mi-N-gl-Y

leaves
(sEe)
locked

in

gOLd
after-
gLOw

are

t
ReMbLiN

g
,;:.:;,

By e. e. cummings

e. e. cummings, 1962.
Photograph: UPI/Bettmann.

Rhythmic Writings

By using musical elements such as timing and rhythm, e. e. cummings tried to control the sound of words. He would stretch out a word such as dreaming in a specific way to produce rhythmic beats.

Think of a single interesting word. It may be one that you like the sound of or one that has special meaning to you. Tap out a beat on your knee or other hard surface while you say the word, stretching it out to follow the rhythm you have created. Write the word down using hyphens or upper- and lowercase letters to show the beats. How does the word look? How do you read it? Is it sounded out long and slow or short and fast? Add words to form a sentence or phrase which will enhance the meaning and rhythmic interest of your piece.

Your completed poem should be composed of words that make your eyes move and your body want to respond to the beat.

MAKING THE CONNECTION

The words of a poem are arranged in lines rather than sentences. The lines can be grouped together and arranged to create a certain meaning and sense of rhythm. The same can be said for the lines and shapes in a piece of art. Kandinsky spaced out a variety of lines and geometric shapes on paper to create a feeling of movement. Both artists disregarded traditional rules of composition to make statements with their rhythmic techniques. The sense of rhythm is so strong in their poems and paintings that music could be added to accompany their works, following along with their patterns of beats.

Ch-ugs and WhiSSSS les

Ch - ug

Ch - ug

up the

      L

    L

  i

h

GOOO eS

the train

while

Whi SSSSS

ling

A

tune

By Lindsey Snyder, grade 5

Georgia O'Keeffe

1887–1986 * AMERICAN

Even as a child growing up on a farm in Sun Prairie, Wisconsin, Georgia O'Keeffe was aware of nature's wonders and had a strong affection for the land. She spent a lot of time outdoors observing the simplest forms of nature. As she grew older, she began collecting nature specimens to study and draw. As an adult, she turned her observations into paintings that showed the world of nature in a new way, up close and personal.

When her family moved to Virginia, O'Keeffe's school principal and art teacher, Elizabeth May Willis, praised O'Keeffe's drawings and encouraged her to go to art school. O'Keeffe went to Chicago to study art when she was sixteen and continued her studies in New York City. There she married a successful photographer and gallery owner, Alfred Stieglitz, who showed her work in his gallery.

O'Keeffe traveled all over the United States seeking inspiration for her paintings. Before her marriage, she had taught art classes to children in Virginia, Texas and New Mexico, and she loved spending time in the Southwest. She felt at home in the wide open space of the desert's vast plains, which held seemingly magical inspiration for her.

Whenever she painted, O'Keeffe magnified simple shapes and forms from nature to emphasize their vitality and uniqueness. In her famous flower paintings, O'Keeffe enlarged the blooms to gigantic proportions, making people looking at the paintings feel as if they were the size of a bumblebee. She said, "When you take a flower in your hand and really look at it, its your world for the moment. I want to give that world to someone else. Most people in the city rush around so, they have no time to look at a flower. I want them to see it whether they want to or not."

Nature's Abstracts

Georgia O'Keeffe looked at nature in a unique way, often enlarging her subjects to give us a different perspective on how to view even the simplest forms in nature. A flower, a leaf or even a shell can be magnified and seen in new ways, emphasizing color, line, pattern, texture, shape and form. This enlargement of forms is a type of *abstraction* in which the identifiable object is simplified, distorted or rearranged according to the artist's ideas.

You will need

several simple objects found in nature
    (flowers, leaves, pinecones, shells, etc.)
newspaper or other material for
    covering tabletop
large sheets of white or colored
    construction paper
colored pastel chalks

Georgia O'Keeffe, 1953. Gelatin silver print, 9½ x 7⁷⁄₁₆" (24 x 19 cm). Amon Carter Museum, Fort Worth. Photograph by Laura Gilpin.

To begin

Examine the painting *Purple Petunias* by O'Keeffe shown here, and try to identify the subject matter in its enlarged form. Notice how the colors fill the picture's space and how each part of the shape is magnified to show details. Select one object from nature such as a flower or leaf for your own drawing. Look for interesting shapes and surface patterns.

Cover your tabletop with newspaper or other protective material. Starting in the center of a large sheet of white or colored construction paper, draw the basic shape of your selected object. Draw an outline of the shape in chalk. Make it large enough to touch the sides and bottom of your paper. If you make a mistake, rub off the chalk and try again. To create interest in the drawing, add a few of the details seen around the object. When the object's basic shape is on paper, start to fill in the page with color. O'Keeffe used a limited palette of colors blended together. This helped enhance the bold shapes and enlarged forms in her works. Try to limit your own use of colors to two or three choices and expand the range by using the various shades and tones of those colors. Use a facial tissue to help to blend the colors together.

The background of the drawing is just as important as the main subject. Use solid colors or designs to complement the main object in the composition.

Variation

Details can be added on top of the pastel chalk drawings with bold pen lines or crosshatched pencil designs. These additions can give the picture added texture. Chalk dipped into water also creates some variation, making bold lines.

Abby Paffrath, grade 5.

Purple Petunias, 1926. Oil on canvas, 15⅞ x 13" (40 x 33 cm).
Collection of The Newark Museum. Bequest of Miss Cora Louise Hartshorn, 1958.

MY HEART SOARS

The beauty of the trees,
the softness of the air,
the fragrance of the grass,
    speaks to me.

The summit of the mountain,
the thunder of the sky,
the rhythm of the sea,
    speaks to me.

The faintness of the stars,
the freshness of the morning,
the dewdrop on the flower,
    speaks to me.

The strength of fire,
the taste of salmon,
the trail of the sun,
and the life that never goes away,
    they speak to me.

And my heart soars.

By Chief Dan George

Chief Dan George

1899–1981 ✳ SALISH, NATIVE AMERICAN

Chief Dan George grew up along the coast of North Vancouver, Canada. He was deeply influenced by the beauty of the area's natural surroundings. As a child, he was fascinated by the marine life around him. He also loved to swim in the ocean and play on the rocks at the shore. The ocean, the mountains and the rivers of his home inspired him to write poetry.

Chief Dan George was also influenced by his culture, that of the Salish tribe of Northwest Coastal Indians. He wanted to hold on to the history of his people and to revive their traditions. Many of his people's customs were lost when missionaries came to his village while he was a young child. Chief Dan George saw the North American Indian's way of life change to fit the teachings of the Christian church. Writing poetry became a way of expressing his memories of earlier times.

My Heart Soars is a book of poetry as well as the name of a poem by Chief Dan George. Like most of his works, the pieces celebrate the lives of North American Indians and the natural world.

Chief Dan George.
Photograph:
UPI/Bettmann.

MAKING THE CONNECTION

The challenge of painting a view of nature or describing it with personal meaning is the focus of the works by O'Keeffe and Chief Dan George. The grass, the trees, the sea, the flowers and the sun each had special meaning in their lives. O'Keeffe was totally inspired by the Southwest desert and its majestic landscape. Chief Dan George tried to bring into focus the magic of Canada's Northwest Coastal region. Both artists believed that the balance of life is reflected in the simple forms of nature. To watch and listen with alert minds and to focus on a variety of nature's forms, is the intent both had for their audiences. Does your environment make you see, feel or think in a special way?

Nature Reflections

Chief Dan George shares with us the special relationship that he has with nature when he tells us that it "speaks to him." By isolating this phrase at the end of each verse, he emphasizes how important his interaction with nature is to him.

To begin

Find a special place outside where you will not be disturbed. What objects in nature speak to you? How does nature inspire you? Does the "summit of the mountain" or the "freshness of the morning" excite your senses or evoke strong emotion?

To write your own nature poem, make a list of observations that appeal to your senses, such as the laughter of a child, the flutter of a butterfly or the excitement of the city. Group together three or four observations to form each *stanza*, or set of related lines in your poem.

Think of a phrase that you can finish each stanza with, as Chief Dan George did when he wrote "my heart soars." Your phrase might be "sings to my heart" or "brings peace to my soul."

Peace From Nature

The flow of the river,
The babbling of a brook,
Brings peace to my soul.

The magnificence of the mountains,
The snow on their peaks,
Brings peace to my soul.

By Sharon Martin, grade 5

31

8

Frank Lloyd Wright

1867–1959 ✳ AMERICAN

Even before her son was born, Frank Lloyd Wright's mother believed he would be a great architect. She was so sure that she hung engravings of cathedrals on his nursery walls. When he was six, she bought him a special set of wooden blocks so he could learn to build structures out of basic shapes like cubes and cylinders. As Frank grew up, he became fascinated with the forms and shapes that nature creates, and he experimented with wood and other natural materials to make forts and houses to play in. As an engineering student, he studied new technologies and apprenticed with established architects in Chicago. His mother was right: over time, Frank learned to combine his love for nature with new technologies and simple shapes and designs to revolutionize American architecture.

In revolt against the fixed designs and rules of traditional architecture, Wright developed a style called *organic architecture*. Using simple shapes and designs, his buildings seem to blend into and grow out of the surrounding landscape. In particular, in Chicago he created a type of home called the *prairie house*. This long, low house with a flat projecting roof was inspired by the flat land of the prairie.

Wright's houses were also revolutionary on the inside. He did not like the small, dark rooms of many of the houses of his time. Inspired by the design of Japanese homes, he opened up the space inside his houses, allowing one room to flow into another with as few dividing walls as possible. He also opened up the inside of his houses to the outside world of nature through the use of many windows and access from most rooms to outdoor porches and balconies. To fit the unique style of his houses and buildings, Wright even created specific furniture and stained glass windows. His favorite color was Cherokee red, which he used freely in many of his designs.

Wright wanted his houses to be homes, havens for the families that lived inside them. Each of the homes he designed reflect a part of the personalities of the people for whom they were built. In his own home, Wright included a special room for a piano, since he loved music and his wife was a musician and composer. He also designed a room for movies and another for dancing.

Frank Lloyd Wright.
Courtesy of The Frank Lloyd Wright Foundation.

Rural and Urban Landscapes

Frank Lloyd Wright once said about architecture "We have no longer an outside and an inside as two separate things. Now the outside may come inside and the inside may and does go outside." This concept can also be seen in many kinds of drawings of buildings, both rural and urban. Small spaces, big buildings and lots of people crowded together are parts of many urban landscapes. Rural life is sparsely populated, with the landscape more spread out and the environment playing a bigger role in how structures are designed.

You will need

magazine pictures of several styles of
    buildings
12 x 18" drawing paper
drawing pencil
ruler, eraser
colored pencils
black and colored felt-tipped markers

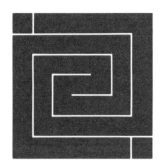

To begin

You can create interesting drawings by comparing the organic and nonorganic nature of urban and rural architecture. Gather pictures from magazines that show the two different styles of living. Discuss what is alike and different about the styles of the buildings in city and rural areas. Think about Wright's organic architectural designs. Did the architects of the buildings in your pictures use the philosophy of Frank Lloyd Wright, with close interaction between the buildings and the environment?

To start your drawing, fold a 12 x 18" piece of paper in half. On one side label the space rural and on the other side label it urban. Now imagine you are one of Frank Lloyd Wright's students and you are asked to design a building in the city and a house in a rural or country area. The environments and the landscapes around your drawings will be just as important as the buildings. Use a ruler to make pencil sketches, making sure the buildings dominate the spaces. After your drawings are done, begin to fill them in and add details with colored pencils or felt-tipped markers. Trace the original pencil lines with black felt-tipped markers to emphasize the outlines. These thick lines will draw attention to details such as windows, trims, columns, arches, staircases and the outside landscape. Use color throughout the picture to give it depth, texture and interest, and to emphasize the surrounding scenery.

Solomon R. Guggenheim Museum, south view, 1943–59. From a slide by Rosenthal Art Slides, Inc., Chicago.

Cameron Abernathy, grade 6.

Variation

Work in small groups to construct a model of one of the participant's buildings using pieces of cardboard or tiny boxes glued together. You could also work in a larger group to construct a school of the future or even an entire city.

SONG OF THE OPEN ROAD

(Part 1 of 15)

Afoot and light-hearted I take to the open road,
Healthy, free, the world before me,
The long brown path before me leading wherever I choose.

Henceforth I ask not good-fortune, I myself
    am good-fortune,
Henceforth I whimper no more, postpone no more, need
    nothing,
Done with indoor complaints, libraries, querulous
    criticisms,
Strong and content I travel the open road.

The earth, that is sufficient,
I do not want the constellations any nearer,
I know they are very well where they are,
I know they suffice for those who belong to them.

(Still here I carry my old delicious burdens,
I carry them, men and women, I carry them with me
    wherever I go,
I swear it is impossible for me to get rid of them,
I am fill'd with them, and I will fill them in return.)

By Walt Whitman

Walt Whitman, 1879.
Photograph:
The Bettmann Archive.

Walt Whitman

1819–1892 * AMERICAN

Walt Whitman is now considered one of America's greatest poets. But in his own time, Whitman's most famous work, *Leaves of Grass,* was at first considered too bizarre for any publishing company to print. Publishers objected to it because it did not have a steady beat or rhyme. Whitman published *Leaves of Grass,* which began as a book containing twelve of his poems, on his own. It was revised and expanded several times during his lifetime to become a reflection of Whitman's life's work.

Whitman was born in West Hills, on Long Island in New York, and was raised in Brooklyn. His restless nature never allowed him to stay at one job long, and he held many positions as a printer and journalist throughout his life. He enjoyed children and taught at several small country schools. However, most of his time was spent reading books, writing and simply wandering throughout the countryside of Long Island and along the busy streets and wharves of New York City. Whitman appreciated all the arts and often attended art exhibitions, the theater and the opera, of which he wrote many reviews. He was also involved in United States politics, often attending debates, lectures and political gatherings. Whitman's lyrical poems express his passion for individual freedom, American democracy and country life.

Worldly Wonders

Whitman traveled city streets and country roads reveling in every part of the natural and constructed worlds around him. In "Song of the Open Road," he expresses some of the joy and wonder he felt while observing the surrounding environment. Can you see designs from nature in the structures around you? Look closely. Can you see the movement of a river, different colors in the earth, the designs in a sea-shell or the shape of the leaves as part of the buildings in your view?

To begin

Similes make a comparison between two things that are not alike using the words like or as. For example, a telephone pole is like a tall sturdy tree in the forest. The brick is as red as the sky at dusk. Make your own comparison between structures you can see and objects from the natural environment. Fill in the blanks:
A _____ is like a _____

Arrange the words of your similes on different lines to create short poems.

MAKING THE CONNECTION

Wright and Whitman are both considered visionary, imaginative artists whose work appeals to the emotions. Their common traits of passion for nature and for the freedom to express themselves in their own unique ways may explain why Whitman was one of Wright's heroes. In many of his poems, Whitman used words to relate his feelings about the importance of people, democracy, the land and the universe. Wright demonstrated his philosophy of the importance of harmony between architecture and nature through his designs, in which buildings' structures seemed to flow in and out of their environments. Both artists used their work to help others focus on the relationship of humanity to the world around us.

The Red Brick

The brick
Is as red as
The sky at dusk

By Brooke Greene, kindergarten

9

Ando Hiroshige

1797–1858 * JAPANESE

Even as a boy, Ando Hiroshige loved to draw. He would take long walks around his home, visiting people in the neighborhood and paying close attention to the way the land looked in different kinds of weather and at different times of day. He would return home to draw and paint the things he saw on his walking adventures. Hiroshige wanted to become an artist, so his father arranged for the boy to take art lessons from a neighborhood amateur. Unfortunately, Hiroshige's parents died when he was only twelve, temporarily halting his dreams of an art career. Hiroshige followed in his father's footsteps to become a firefighter. But he continued to study art seriously, and when his children were grown, he became a professional printmaker.

Hiroshige went on to be one of Japan's most popular printmakers. He created a kind of print called *ukiyo-e*, which means "pictures of the floating world." These prints show the fleeting moments of everyday life of the people of Japan. They show people on the street, travelers along the road and actors in the theater. Because the prints were inexpensive to make, nearly everyone could afford to buy and enjoy them.

Hiroshige's prints were unusual partly because he was one of the first Japanese artists to create ukiyo-e prints of the landscape alone. He loved to paint broad, open scenes with the forces of nature upon them. His works captured the seasons of Japan, all types of weather and the mysterious quality of moonlight on the land. Hiroshige had his own style of printmaking as well as painting. He did not fill his landscapes with details, preferring instead to suggest forms and atmosphere with broad areas of color rather than sharply defining lines. As a result, he became known for his "sweeping brush."

At the time Hiroshige was working, Americans and Europeans were just beginning to become aware of Japanese art. Artists such as Edgar Degas of France and James Whistler of the United States were fascinated by the style and composition of Hiroshige's prints. They began to experiment with the asymmetrical arrangements, flat areas of color and delicate lines that they admired in Hiroshige's and other Japanese printmakers' work.

Pictures of the Floating World

Many Japanese printmakers referred to their artworks as "pictures of the floating world." Hiroshige expressed this idea in his printed pictures as well. He created images of nature and quiet moments from everyday life by carving designs on a slab of wood called a plate. He painted bold colors of ink on the carved plate, placed paper on the inked surface, and, after applying pressure, removed the paper to reveal a finished print.

Utagawa Kunisada, **Memorial Portrait of Hiroshige,** 1858.

Hodogaya Station, from the Tokeido Series, 1832–34. Collection of Bertha and Mitchel Siegel, Santa Fe, New Mexico.

You will need

9 x 12" pieces of drawing paper
Styrofoam trays of various sizes (used in supermarket meat and vegetable packaging)
scissors
toothpicks, sticks or other tools for making impressions
newspapers or other table covering
tempera or acrylic paints
paintbrushes
water cups for rinsing
spray bottle filled with water
spoon, brayer or rolling pin

To begin

Artists create prints using plates made from a variety of materials, including wood, plastic and metal. They can use these plates more than once — many times, in fact — to create a series of similar prints. This series is called an edition. You can create a single print or an entire edition using a plate made of Styrofoam.

Think of a simple form in nature such as a bird, butterfly, flower, fish or tree. Draw an image of this form on a 9 x 12" piece of paper. Use a variety of types of lines to create your drawing, some squiggly, some straight, some thick and some thin. This will create interest in your design. Use a pair of scissors to cut the curved edges off one of the Styrofoam trays, leaving a flat surface or plate on which to work. Place your drawing on top of the foam plate. Trace over your drawing with a pencil, making indented lines on the foam. After all of your lines are transferred to the piece of foam, remove the paper and trace over the lines again using a toothpick or other carving tool to make them bolder.

The foam plate is ready for inking with either tempera or acrylic paints. Cover a flat working surface such as a tabletop with newspaper or other material. You can paint the entire surface of the plate with one color or use a limited palette of two or three colors as in the prints by Hiroshige.

Emily Erb, grade 6. Photograph courtesy of the 1992–93 Crayola® Dream-Makers™ program, Binney & Smith, Inc.

Matsuo Bashō

1644–1694 ✳ JAPANESE

Picture yourself floating on the waves of a lake in summer. The simple words of Matsuo Bashō's poem paint a scene of great peacefulness. Vivid images of nature are one feature of a type of poetry known as haiku, and Matsuo Bashō is the most noted early writer of Japanese haiku. He has been called The First Great Master of Haiku, a type of Japanese poetry that has three brief lines. When Matsuo was about twelve years old, he became a page, or personal servant, to the son of a lord named Yoshitada. They formed a friendship and together studied haiku with one of the most respected teachers of the day. When Yoshitada died, Bashō moved to Tokyo and began writing haiku seriously. He became a recluse, living in a hut given to him by his followers so that he could study nature without distractions. He said, "Learn of the pine from the pine; learn of the bamboo from the bamboo. In writing, do not let a hair's breadth separate yourself from the subject. Speak your mind directly; go to it without wandering thoughts."

Matsuo Bashō.

You must print your picture before the paint dries. If the paints dries before you are finished, use a spray bottle filled with water to mist over the foam board. Place a blank piece of 9 x 12" paper on top of the foam plate centering the paper on the plate as best as possible, and press firmly. You can use a spoon, brayer (a printer's inking roller), or rolling pin or your hands to smooth and press the paper on the foam. Remove the paper by pulling it off the plate from one corner, and your print is complete.

Variation

Simple figures can be cut from foam to create shaped printing plates. Several of these shapes can be printed on a large piece of paper to make a pattern. Each time you print you will need to add paint to the foam shapes, which can be used several times and saved for future use.

Summer in the world;
Floating on the waves
Of the lake.

By Matsuo Bashō

Poems of the Floating World

Haiku is a form of Japanese poetry that has three concise lines. Each haiku generally contains a total of seventeen syllables, with five syllables on the first line, seven on the second and five again on the last line. Original haiku often lose the five - seven - five pattern when translated to English. Although it is not necessary to use this pattern of syllables when composing a haiku, it can be fun to try in your first attempts.

To begin

Write a haiku of a floating world or a passing moment in nature. Start by finding a place in the country or in your neighborhood where you can observe nature. Look for an image that appeals to your senses. Can you hear a bird singing or the wind blowing through the grass? Do you see the sun rising over the mountains or stars shining above a building? Do you see flowers dancing in a field or garden?

Write down simple yet vivid phrases of three or four words each that capture a passing moment about your subject. Choose three lines to form your haiku. It is sometimes fun to clap out the syllables in each line to see if you have the five - seven - five arrangement, although the emphasis in your work should be on the meaning and emotion behind the words you choose.

Flow-ers free, danc-ing
In a gar-den so peace-ful
Twirl-ing, laugh-ing, gay

By Maria Vasquez, grade 1

MAKING THE CONNECTION

Hiroshige and Bashō both used their art to express fleeting moments in nature. Both of their art forms, landscape printing and haiku, use simple designs or words to create pictures that observers must use their imagination to complete. These images often show a sense of harmony between people and the natural world.

A landscape is a scene that should be viewed from a distance in order to grasp the total picture, such as the scheme of waves or floating hills. Tiny human figures on mountain paths may appear as no more important than rocks, trees or waterfalls. Landscape prints are representations of these elements of nature. Haiku poems are also usually symbolic expressions of the elements in nature. A haiku's short lines and carefully chosen words work together to help readers understand something about themselves and their world.

Ask yourself, as did Japanese artists and philosophers of long ago, Is the world of nature only rolling hills and immense continents, or is it also the world of imagination within each of us?

Flowers free, dancing (5 claps or syllables)
In a garden so peaceful (7 claps or syllables)
Twirling, laughing, gay (5 claps or syllables)

Since the English translation of Bashō's "Summer in the World" haiku has lost the original's five - seven - five pattern, it is not a helpful example to follow in your own writing. It is certainly worth sharing, though, for the clear picture it paints of a floating world.

10

Nike Davies

1951– * NIGERIAN

Nike Davies was born in the small village of Ogide in Nigeria. Her father was a farmer as well as a gifted drummer and leather craftsmen. Nike had a difficult childhood. Her mother died when she was only six years old, leaving her responsible for many of the household chores. In addition to cooking, cleaning and looking after her younger brother, Nike learned traditional African craft skills from her grandmother. She learned to process raw cotton and make the traditional *oja*, or long strips of cotton used for carrying babies on mothers' backs. In school she learned to make textured designs on cotton fabric and to use the indigo plant for fabric dye.

Although the young Davies felt these tasks were mere household chores, she showed a talent for designing and decorating fabric. Even as a teenager she was able to sell her richly patterned and embroidered pieces. Soon she began to dream of escaping the hard work of village life to become somebody in the world. At just sixteen, Davies ran away from home to join a traveling theater group. It was in this group that she met her husband, Twins Seven Seven, a man who encouraged her to develop her gifts for music, dance and art. He taught her how to draw and create the traditional decorative fabric designs produced by batik, a process that uses the application of wax and dyes to paint pictures.

Davies' batik designs became increasingly sophisticated as she began combining traditional African patterns and themes with those from her own imagination. Drawing imagery from African history, myths, dreams and everyday life, Davies continues to work in her home in Nigeria, creating innovative batik designs renowned throughout the world.

Images in Batik

Batik artists from around the world share their cultural heritage through the designs they create on cloth. *Batik* is a method of dyeing fabric that involves brushing a wax design on a piece of cloth. When the fabric is dipped in dye, all but the part covered in wax changes color, producing the desired pattern. Decorative patterns can tell stories of each culture. Such is the case with Nigerian artist Nike Davies.

You will need

heavy-weight drawing paper or heavy
    brown wrapping paper
wax crayons
newspaper
sink or tub of water
transparent watercolor paints (tube or pan)
water cups for rinsing
paintbrushes
iron and ironing board
wax paper

To begin

You can produce the crackled lines that are characteristic of batik by painting transparent watercolors over the heavy lines of wax crayons.

Begin by drawing a simple outlined design with a light-colored crayon (yellow or white) on heavy paper. Your drawing can be a design of interesting shapes, or it can be a drawing of a person, plant or animal. Remember to draw outlines only; do not fill large areas with color. After the design is complete, go over the lines with crayon. Make the lines thick. Heavier lines will give a better batik effect.

Nike Davies. Photograph © Juliet Highet.

Worshipping of Ogun: God of Irm.
Photograph © Juliet Highet.

Crumple your paper into a ball. This will create cracks in the drawn crayon lines. Open the paper ball. Soak the paper in a tub of water for a few seconds, then flatten it out on a stack of newspapers. The wet paper can tear easily, so be careful. You can begin to add color to the white areas of your design with dark watercolor paints. Wet your paintbrush in the water cup, swirl the brush around in a color of the pan watercolor, and apply the color to your paper. The paints will soak into the cracked crayon lines of the wet paper to create a crinkle effect. The background can be painted with several colors and designs. The paints will not mix with the crayon, so the light crayon lines will help define the batik pattern.

Once the paper is dry, use an iron to flatten and smooth out the drawn lines. *Note: Ask for an adult's help when using an iron or other electrical devices. An adult should always be present to make sure the iron is*

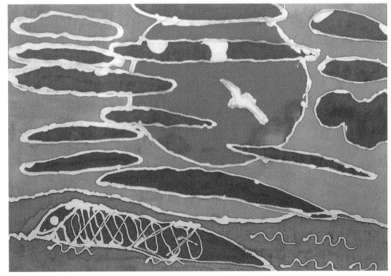

Alex Headly, grade 5.

used safely and properly. Put your drawing on an ironing board and place a piece of wax paper on top of the drawing. The iron will glide more easily and will not be damaged by the wax paper. You may put newspaper under your drawing to protect the ironing board if you want. The heat of the iron will melt the wax paper on the crayon and into the crinkle lines, creating a smooth surface. *Be careful not to overheat the paper. Overheating could cause the paper to catch on fire.* Your crayon batik will have the crinkled look of a fabric batik, with a colorful drawing of your own design.

Variation

The same method used on paper can be done using cotton muslin fabric and melted crayons. The crayons can be heated in a special crayon melter (available at art supply stores), and the melted crayons can be painted on top of the drawn pencil designs. Use old paintbrushes that can be thrown away or saved for this purpose only. When crayon wax is cool and dry, follow instructions for crinkling, soaking and painting the fabric, just as with the paper drawings. The finished fabric design can be stretched on an embroidery hoop to give it a frame.

Langston Hughes.
Photograph:
Springer/Bettmann
Film Archive.

Langston Hughes

1902–1967 ✳ AFRICAN AMERICAN

Langston Hughes was born in an era of fierce racial discrimination. In the early twentieth century, African Americans typically had no formal schooling. But Hughes's family members were all educated and proud of their racial heritage. They communicated this pride to Langston who, in turn, devoted his life to promoting the accomplishments and potential of all African Americans.

Hughes's father studied law but was unable to become a lawyer because of discrimination in the United States. He was eventually able to practice law in Mexico City. When Hughes was a young child, his mother was forced to leave him in the custody of his grandmother in Kansas while she looked for employment. Hughes's grandmother was a wonderful storyteller. She would set him on her lap and tell long, intriguing tales. At the age of fourteen, Hughes was able to return to his mother, and she introduced him to poetry. She sometimes wrote poetry and enjoyed reciting long verses to her son.

When he was in high school, Hughes began writing his own poetry. He wrote pieces for the class newspaper and was bestowed the title of Class Poet. Verses constantly filled his mind, and he would write his thoughts down on anything he could find.

Hughes experimented with a variety of poetry forms including lyric verse, blank verse and dialect. Much of his poetry came out of African-American traditions. He was interested in jazz and the blues and even wrote the lyrics for a musical play. After college, he lived for a time in New York City's Harlem. There he joined the many writers, artists and musicians who took part in a cultural revolution known as the Harlem Renaissance.

Throughout his life, Hughes worked tirelessly to educate Americans about the evils of racism. His poetry and short stories often tell about the difficult conditions of life for African Americans. He wrote histories of black culture for young black readers to promote racial pride. He also traveled throughout the South, reading his work to African-American students to encourage them to achieve their goals and dreams despite discrimination.

DREAMS

Hold fast to dreams
For if dreams die
Life is a broken-winged bird
That cannot fly.

Hold fast to dreams
For when dreams go
Life is a barren field
Frozen with snow.

By Langston Hughes

MAKING THE CONNECTION

Dreams can be visions or ideals that people work to achieve, dreams can conjure up important personal images that people may want to hold on to. Davies has dreams of keeping alive the African traditions of her people and she sometimes sketches actual images that appeared to her while sleeping to use as themes for her artwork. Hughes envisioned African Americans aspiring to their dreams despite racial discrimination. His poetry tells them to "Hold fast to dreams . . . ." Both artists may make you think about your own dreams and how you can use them to share your personal visions with others.

Dream Visions

Langston Hughes used *metaphors* to create interest in his poem "Dreams." A metaphor makes a comparison between objects or ideas, suggesting a similarity between them without using the words *like* or *as*, which are found in similes. For example, Hughes tells us that "Life is a broken-winged bird that can not fly," and "Life is a barren field frozen with snow."

Metaphors are especially useful for writing poems that explore our dreams, which are often filled with vivid images. Calling life a "barren field" helps readers really see and feel the sadness of lost dreams.

To begin

Do you ever dream about what you will be one day? Possibly you dream about what it would be like to live in a clean and healthy environment where all animals are protected from extinction. You might dream about living in a world where there is peace, love and harmony among all people. You might have visions of someone or something special to you.

Write down the highlights or subjects of your dream. Next to these main ideas and images, use your imagination to write things that they remind you of. Were there clouds in your dream? Were they soft white marshmallows floating through sky? Was there a hero in your dream who was a strong, solid rock?

Write a dream poem using the metaphors you have formed.

Sometimes

Sometimes I dream about
traveling to a land far away

Sometimes I dream about
playing in a castle on a cloud

Sometimes I dream about
being a princess in a beautiful dress

Most of all, I dream about
marrying a prince

By Carol Dellaney, grade 2

Pieter Bruegel

1525–1569 ✴ FLEMISH

Pieter Bruegel the Elder was born in Flanders, near the border of Holland and Belgium. He was called "the elder" to distinguish him from his sons and grandsons who also became painters. During Bruegel's teens, he worked as an apprentice to an engraver. There he learned to create prints affordable to the average person that illustrated funny and instructive stories from everyday life and the Bible.

Bruegel left Flanders for formal art training in Italy, where he discovered the beauty of landscape in the Italian countryside and the breathtaking mountain ranges of the Alps. When he returned to Flanders, he began painting the landscape of his own homeland and pictures of the common people, or peasants, who lived and worked on it. His paintings show peasants in the countryside during different seasons of the year, children playing games and rustic celebrations such as wedding feasts. In *The Harvesters,* Bruegel captures the golden glow of the summer heat and the bounty of the land. Some of the people in the scene work at harvesting the field, while others sit beneath a tree, eating the fruits of their labors. The scene is one of peace and bounty, of people working hard in harmony with nature. Bruegel's paintings are also often filled with fun and humor. One man in *The Harvesters* has become so full that he has had to loosen his trousers and has fallen asleep under a tree. Bruegel lived only forty years. Most of his works that have survived are the drawings he did for engravers early in his life. Only about forty of his paintings can be found today. His sons, Jan and Pieter the Younger, tried to carry on their father's work but never matched his greatness.

Harvest Celebration

The feeling of putting in a hard day's work and the enjoyment of relaxation at the end of the day are parts of everyday life that Pieter Bruegel expressed in his paintings. His colors make rhythmic patterns that give a feeling of movement, just as there is a rhythm to the work of a harvest. He painted large crowds, yet each individual is clearly portrayed with loving details that reveal the artist's respect and affection for the workers.

You will need

newspaper or other material for
    covering tabletop
watercolor paper
drawing pencil
watercolor paints
watercolor paintbrushes, several sizes
water cups for rinsing
colored felt-tipped markers

Pieter Bruegel.
Photograph: Graphische
Sammlung Albertina, Vienna.

The Harvesters (July),
1565. Oil on wood, 46½
x 63¼" (118 x 161 cm).
The Metropolitan
Museum of Art, Rogers
Fund, 1919. (19.164)

Cari Lewis, grade 4.

To begin

Paint your own harvest celebration picture. Discuss what should be in your picture to set the mood for a harvest scene. Think of what you know about farm life to help create a setting for your picture: the work of the harvesters is very hard. Many people work together to harvest a crop. Some people might be working while others are resting.

After you establish your idea for a picture, draw it on watercolor paper. First sketch the general layout lightly using a pencil. You might choose to draw several people close up or far away in the background. To prepare for painting, think about the season of your picture and what is being harvested. This will help set the mood or feeling. Think about what the people in your painting will be doing and add tiny details to indicate it. Begin painting your picture using watercolor paints. If you want dark colors, which give shadows and depth put a lot of paint on your brush. If you want lighter colors, add water to your brush. Watercolor paints dry fast. Once the painting is done, you can go back over your pencil lines with the tips of felt-tipped markers to emphasize the details. The markers will make your painting bolder and give it a feeling of being alive.

Wendell Berry

1934– * AMERICAN

Wendell Berry is an organic farmer, philosopher and poet who lives with his wife and two children on a farm along the Kentucky River. His writing reflects his active interest in environmental issues (particularly his concerns for the land and its conservation) and American family life. He has written many essays and novels but is most satisfied with his poetry. He believes it is his "least-flawed work." He says, "Learning to write poetry helped me to see farming as a way of life, not merely as a scientific manipulation of techniques and quantities." His poem "Sowing the Seed" celebrates the close relationship that develops between a farmer and the world of nature.

Wendell Berry, 1975. Reprinted with permission from *The Courier-Journal.*

SOWING THE SEED

Sowing the seed,
my hand is one with the earth.

Wanting the seed to grow,
my mind is one with the light.

Hoeing the crop,
my hands are one with the rain.

Having cared for the plants,
my mind is one with the air.

Hungry and trusting,
my mind is one with the earth.

Eating the fruit,
my body is one with the earth.

By Wendell Berry

A Harvest of Images

Harvest is a time for celebration. After having planted and cared for the crops, farmers can now reap the fruits of their labor. Lyric poetry offers an effective way to express the joy, satisfaction and relief that come with the harvest.

A lyric poem is a short work that allows the feelings and emotions of a poet to be vividly stated. Writers sometimes refer to themselves in these poems by using personal pronouns such as I, me and my. Which of these words does Wendell Berry use in his poem "Sowing the Seed"? Other times you might not actually see such references, but you would still know that the poets were writing about what they saw, felt and thought.

To begin

Write a lyric poem about something you achieved that made you want to shout for joy. Tell about your accomplishment. Why is it important to you? How did it impact other people? Thoughtfully consider the words you will write, and place them on paper in a meaningful way. Help readers feel and hear all the emotions that you felt at the moment of success.

The Saviour

I saved a tree
standing
tall and proud
Reusing
a piece of paper
once,
twice,
three times !!!

By David Kooper

MAKING THE CONNECTION

Bruegel's painting and Berry's poem reveal the importance of the land through the labors of its people. Both works give us a clear view of the work involved during harvest time and the celebration of bountiful crops. Each artist tells of hard labor and the toils and benefits of working the land. Have you ever helped grow a garden or watched someone else tend one? Such experiences can help us understand the farmers of today and how the food we eat starts on the long road to our tables.

Henry Ossawa Tanner

1859–1937 ✳ AFRICAN AMERICAN

At the age of thirteen, Henry Ossawa Tanner decided to become an artist. He had been walking with his father in Philadelphia's Fairmount Park when he saw a man sketching a portrait of a person. His eyes widened as he watched the transformation of the portrait on paper. From that day on, he began teaching himself to draw by sketching on anything he could find, scraps of paper, pieces of wood, even old cardboard.

As a young man, Tanner wanted to study art professionally but found it difficult to obtain art lessons because he was an African American. He was finally accepted into the Pennsylvania Academy of Fine Arts, where he received encouragement from the noted artist and educator Thomas Eakins. Tanner could not support himself as an artist in America, however, so he decided to move to Paris, at that time the center of the art world. It was less expensive to live there than in Philadelphia, and there was less racial discrimination. In Paris Tanner's paintings won many awards and became very popular.

Tanner painted a wide variety of subjects, including religious images, portraits and landscapes. He also painted subjects and scenes from everyday life, called genre paintings. *The Banjo Lesson* is a genre painting of Southern life in the United States. In Tanner's time too many genre works depicted African Americans in comic stereotypes. With *The Banjo Lesson* Tanner wanted to create a dignified image of African-American life, of knowledge being passed from one generation to another.

Thomas Eakins, **Portrait of Henry O. Tanner,** 1902. Oil on canvas, 24 1/16 x 20 1/4" (61 x 51 cm). The Hyde Collection, Glens Falls, New York.

Musical Stories

In *genre* paintings, artists show simple scenes of daily life. In *The Banjo Lesson,* an adult is teaching a young person to play a musical instrument. Here the banjo is the focus of the picture. Notice how both people are concentrating closely on the instrument. Can you "hear" the notes as the young boy plucks the strings of the banjo? Can you imagine how the music might sound?

You will need

sketch paper
pencil
materials of various shapes or capable of
    producing interesting sounds (rubber
    bands, cellophane, aluminum plates,
    wire, pieces of metal or wood, plastic
    bottles, corks, various containers, etc.)
cardboard
scissors
tape, wire, glue or other materials for
    fastening objects together
tempera or acrylic paints
paintbrushes
water cups for rinsing

To begin

What sort of instruments do musicians play? Can you name some? Look at pictures of instruments you might see in a band or orchestra. Choose one you would like build as a sculpture. You can work with a small group of two or three people to construct one instrument or an entire ensemble.

Draw the instrument on sketch paper. Show the details and shape of the instrument. Experiment with different shapes and sizes. Sort out your various gathered materials and decide how they can be used in relation to your drawing.

Do any of the objects have shapes which are similar to the shape of your instrument? How can these objects be used together or separately to build an instrument? Start building a basic frame or shape for your instrument. Fasten the various found items together with tape, wire, glue, or other appropriate materials. If you need additional shapes, try cutting and adding pieces of cardboard.

Once the basic form is completed, begin to add details which will make it look like an instrument. Some materials have interesting sounds and can be used to create sound effects. Your instrument may be painted a solid background color. After it is dry, use tempera or acrylic paints to add designs or details to the instrument. The completed instruments can be hung from the ceiling or arranged on top of a table as an imaginative still life. The purpose of this activity is not to produce a real musical instrument that plays, but to create an artistic interpretation of an instrument. Try being creative and use the musical instruments as subjects for a still-life painting or drawing.

Variation

After you have completed the basic construction of your instrument you might want to use papier mâché to cover the outside of the sculpture. This will make the structure sturdy and will create a smooth outside surface. Begin with 1"-thick strips of newspaper and a liquefied mixture of white glue and water. The strips of paper can be about 6 to 8" long. Dip a newspaper strip into the glue and water mixture. Remove excess glue and wrap the strip around your sculpture. Layer the strips on the structure in smooth pieces. Once dry the papier-mâché sculpture can be painted and decorated.

The Banjo Lesson, 1893. Oil on canvas. Hampton University Museum, Hampton, Virginia.

3rd grade group project.

Carl Sandburg

1878–1967 * AMERICAN

Carl Sandburg has been called the voice of America. His restless nature took him all over middle America, traveling as a hobo, as an odd-jobs man, as an author and lecturer. Wherever he went, he listened to and learned from working Americans. It was their lives he wanted to capture in his poetry, prose and folksongs.

Sandburg was one of seven children born to Swedish immigrant parents. His mother and father worked hard to make a living for the large family, In Carl's early teens, he had to leave school to help support the family. He drove a milk wagon along country roads in all kinds of weather and worked as a tinsmith, as a painter's apprentice, in a barber shop and at many other odd jobs.

Because he had served briefly in the Spanish-American War, Sandburg received free tuition to Lombard College for one year. He stayed two and a half more years, during which one of his professors encouraged him to develop his interest in writing. It was not until Sandburg was thirty-six years old that some of his poems were published in a poetry magazine and he began to be known and recognized. He was dubbed the Chicago Poet because his early poems celebrated the power and people of that city. In these poems, he coined the phrase the City of the Big Shoulders.

Sandburg went on to write several volumes of poetry about the lives of working Americans. He tried to capture the language of the working man using *free verse,* or verse that does not rhyme or have regular meter, slang. He had a keen ear for rhythm, and his writing has been described as flowing like a musical composition. His poem "Jazz Fantasia" includes words that describe the sound of music, but the sounds and syllables of the words themselves also have a rhythm all their own — just like music. At forty-two, Sandburg began collecting and singing American folk songs. He traveled all over the country playing his guitar, singing folk songs and sharing his poetry. He also appeared on television and on the radio, where he became very popular.

Sandburg is also known for two brilliant biographies of Abraham Lincoln. *Abraham Lincoln: The Prairie Years* and *Abraham Lincoln: The War Years* took him thirty years to write. *The War Years* won him a Pulitzer Prize.

Carl Sandburg. Photograph: The Bettmann Archive.

JAZZ FANTASIA

Drum on your drums, batter on
    your banjoes,
sob on the long cool winding saxophones.
Go to it, O jazzmen.

Sling your knuckles on the bottoms
    of the happy
tin pans, let your trombones ooze,
    and go husha-
husha-hush with the slippery sand-paper.

Moan like an autumn wind high in the
    lonesome treetops, moan soft like
you wanted somebody terrible, cry like a
    racing car slipping away from a
motorcycle cop, bang-bang! you jazzmen,
    bang altogether drums, traps,
banjoes, horns, tin cans — make two
    people fight on the top of a stairway
and scratch each other's eyes in a clinch
    tumbling down the stairs.

Can the rough stuff . . . now a Mississippi
    steamboat pushes up the night
river with a hoo-hoo-hoo-oo . . . and the
    green lanterns calling to the high
soft stars . . . a red moon rides on the
    humps of the low river hills . . .
go to it, O jazzmen.

By Carl Sandburg

Rhythmic Ramblings

Rhythm is created by the syllables of language and by the beats and patterns in everyday life, such as the sound of a swing in motion. It can also be produced by the location of words on a paper. Rhythm can stir up emotions by the different moods it can create. Sometimes rhythm is smooth but other times it wanders.

The words in Carl Sandburg's poems often flow with a rhythm that almost makes you want to tap your foot. This rhythmic quality plus his vivid descriptions of sound give his works a musical feeling.

What sounds do you "hear" in "Jazz Fantasia"? What words does Sandburg use to describe these sounds? What instruments and other things are making musical sounds? Can you tap out a rhythm to this poem?

To begin

Take a walk through your town, city or park. What sounds do you hear? Listen to the rhythm of a chain spinning as a bike moves along. Does the sound of roller skates turning on pavement create rhythm? Can you hear the high trill of a bird singing, producing a rapid beat? Maybe you hear the rhythm of someone playing a musical instrument such as a drum or banjo, as in "Jazz Fantasia."

Decide if you want the tone of your poem to be lively, using short, fast beats, or whether you want the mood to be sad or somber, using longer beats. Think about where you will place the words on your paper to create these rhythms.

Select for your poem one of the subjects you encounter on your walk that produces a rhythm. Make a list of words and phrases that describes your observations.

MAKING THE CONNECTION

Jazz, which originated in the United States near the end of the 1800s was a great influence on the work of Tanner and Sandburg. It was the style of music that best expressed for them the emotion and feeling of the time. The sounds and rhythm of Jazz can be "heard" and "felt" in their poetry and paintings. In Tanner and Sandburg's heyday, there was a feeling of excitement in America's cities which were bursting with the new energy of industries being developed. We get a sense of this vitality when Sandburg writes of a Mississippi steamboat pushing up the night river or describes "a race car slipping away from a motorcycle cop, bang-bang!" The times were also simple in their own way as Tanner, shows us in *The Banjo Lesson*, where a moment is being spent with a special person and the teaching of music.

Include all your senses. What do you see? What are all the sounds you hear? How do things feel to touch?

It helps to have a musical instrument such as a tambourine, a set of maracas or drums to tap out the rhythm of your poem. If you cannot find a musical instrument, rap your fingers on a hard surface or pat your leg as you write. Will you create a smooth beat or an irregular rhythm?

The Swing

The wind moves the lonely swing
back and forth
back and forth
back and forth

The child moves the happy swing
back and forth
back and forth
back and forth

Kindergarten class poem

13

Helen Cordero

1915-1994 ✴ COCHITI PUEBLO INDIAN

When she was a little girl, Helen Cordero would sit for hours listening to the stories of her grandfather, Santiago Quintana. He would tell legends of her ancestors and her New Mexico home, the Cochiti Pueblo. Quintana would talk about "the little people;" small clay figures that represent the grandfathers and grandmothers of long ago. These figures were called "singing mothers" because they were used to tell tribal stories of the ancestors, or "old ones," to the children.

Cordero learned the art of working with clay from her mother and grandmother. They taught her how to make beautiful pots with hand-painted designs. Using these skills, Cordero revived the tradition of the storyteller dolls, referring to examples found in ancient tribal ruins as models.

Cordero's figures come in all shapes and sizes. When the eyes of a storyteller are closed, the figure is said to be thinking; when its mouth is open, it is singing. Most of her figures are constructed from clay and decorated in the traditional colors of red, black, beige and terra-cotta. She displays the storytellers by surrounding them with a large number of children, each with its own distinct features and facial expression.

"All of my potteries come out of my heart. They're my little people. I talk to them and they're singing. If you're listening you can hear them," Cordero has said.

Making storytellers since the 1960s, Cordero has handed down the art to all the members of her family.

Katie Mallouk, grade 3.

Stories in Clay

Older generations in all cultures have passed down stories and legends to their children. For some Native North American Indians, the storyteller figurine has been used as a symbol of their ancestors and as a vehicle for retelling the histories of their people. Storytellers are often displayed surrounded by the smaller figures of children listening to the stories of their people. Making these figurines is one way to help keep alive the traditions of the ancient ways.

You will need

oil cloth or butcher paper to cover the
    work surface
clay (low-fire for use with kiln or
    self-hardening)
cup of water
sponge
tools to shape details (pencil, knife,
    clay tools)
earth color acrylic paints (black, brown,
    beige, terra-cotta)
pictures of traditional storyteller figurines

Helen Cordero. Denver Museum of Natural History. Photograph by Dudley Smith, 1979

To begin

Think of a story you would like to tell. It might be one a parent or grandparent has told you about something that happened in your family. It might be one you make up. Storyteller figures can be made from a variety of clays, such as firing clay, self-hardening clay or oil-based modeling clay. The Cochiti Pueblo Indians have traditionally used the rich clay near their pueblo.

Cover a flat work surface with oil cloth or butcher paper. Create a *cylinder* or tube shape, by rolling out a piece of clay. Split the tube shape up the middle to make legs. Pull out a piece of clay to form the head. The arms can be made by attaching a roll of clay around the body. Use your fingers or a sponge dipped in water to smooth the surface of the clay and help join pieces together. Once the figurine's basic form is made, start the process over again and make smaller versions to represent the children listening to the storyteller. The clay children may sit on the lap, arms and legs of the larger figure, which is traditionally seated. The smaller figures should be securely attached to the storyteller. Study pictures of storytellers to get ideas for ways to make the arms, legs and face for your figure. Pictures can also help you decide what kind of designs you would like to paint on the figures.

Story Teller, 1969. Earthenware, slipped and painted, height 10¾" (27 cm). U.S. Department of the Interior, Indian Arts and Crafts Board. (Cat. W–70.44.1)

While you are making the figures, think about the story or legend your storyteller is relating. The stories are meant to be spoken out loud, not read. The words of the story could have their own rhythm and "paint" vivid pictures. Share your story with others.

Once your clay is completely dry or fired, paint designs and features for the faces on your figurines. Look at some of the designs that Helen Cordero created on her storyteller. Create your own designs with the same basic patterns and colors used by the Cochiti Pueblo Indians.

Henry Wadsworth Longfellow

1807–1882 ✳ AMERICAN

Henry Wadsworth Longfellow knew success at an early age. He published his first poem at just thirteen years old and went to college when he was only fifteen. He had a passion for learning and did exceptionally well in school. By the time he was a senior in college, Longfellow knew that he wanted to become a famous writer. In a letter home he wrote, "If I can ever rise in the world, it must be by the exercise of my talents in the wide field of literature."

Longfellow began writing essays and short stories for magazines, then went on to explore other forms of writing such as ballads, sonnets, narratives and prose. When asked by the college he attended to become a professor of modern languages, he traveled to Europe to learn Spanish, French, Italian and German. The wide variety of literature he read from these countries influenced his writing, but he was also inspired by memories of growing up in Maine. The sea and nearby forests, family life around the fire and North American Indian lore and history were the subject matter of some of his most popular poetic works, including "The Song of Hiawatha" and "Evangeline."

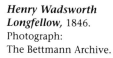

Henry Wadsworth Longfellow, 1846.
Photograph:
The Bettmann Archive.

THE ARROW AND THE SONG

I shot an arrow into the air,
It fell to earth, I knew not where;
For, so swiftly it flew, the sight
Could not follow it in its flight.

I breathed a song into the air,
It fell to earth, I knew not where;
For who has sight so keen and strong,
That it can follow the flight of song?

Long, long afterward, in an oak
I found the arrow, still unbroke;
And the song, from beginning to end,
I found again in the heart of a friend.

By Henry Wadsworth Longfellow

Songs from the Heart

Have you ever heard a story or poem that lingered in your mind for a long time? Did it create rhythms, like music? Have you ever listened to a song that reminded you of someone or someplace special? Did it take you on a journey, as a poem can? Poets often write from the heart about experiences they recall from other times, or about things that touch their emotions in the present. Creating poetry about important personal memories and feelings can give the writer a sense of peace and freedom.

In "The Arrow and the Song," can you "see" the arrow shooting through the air? How do you think Longfellow felt about his friend in the poem? What important things is Longfellow telling us about friendship?

"The Arrow and the Song" is written in quatrain form. A *quatrain* is a verse form containing four lines that do not necessarily have a definite pattern or rhyme arrangement. Longfellow used *couplets,* two lines that rhyme, to build the quatrain.

To begin

Listen to North American Indian flute music (or other music with a soft melody) as you create a poem from your heart about someone, something or someplace special to you. The music's rhythm may help you relax. It may also flow into the poem, or song from the heart, that you are writing.

Start by thinking about a subject you would like to write about. Make a list of descriptive words about your subject, and write rhyming words next to them. It sometimes helps to go through the alphabet and change the first one or two letters of a word to discover the words that rhyme with it. For instance, if your subject is the sun and one of the descriptive words is round, you could list bound, found, ground, hound and mound.

Play with the words to form one couplet, then another. Think of constructing lines that rhyme as a puzzle. When putting together a puzzle, you try to connect pieces; in a couplet you try to connect words that sound alike. It is important that the couplets make sense as well as rhyme. Once you have composed two couplets, put them together to form a quatrain. Try to write at least two quatrains to complete the poem.

Go back and add descriptive words or phrases which will add power to your writing. For instance, instead of writing that the sun is round, add words that stimulate your senses, such as fiery, orange, blinding or blistering the sky. *Imagery,* or the use of figurative language that appeals to the senses, allows your audience to see your vision more clearly.

MAKING THE CONNECTION

Memories of people, events or things can be brought to life through stories, pictures, songs and poetry. Artists and poets often take visions from their memories and put them into forms to share with others. In Longfellow's poem an arrow and a song which were lost for a while are found and brought to mind again, much as a forgotten memory might be rekindled. The poem might remind readers of precious things they have given up or lost and unexpectedly found. Or it might cause a pang of emotion by recalling some gift from "the heart of a friend." Stories handed down by Cordero's storyteller dolls bring back memories of times long ago and help keep alive the traditions of generations long gone. Remembering the past can help people today to understand and celebrate their heritage. Both the artist and poet create works that help us think about and express our own memories.

The Shooting Star

When the sun went down,
As I was sitting under the sky,
A bright little star
Went shooting by.

By Jeff Watkins, grade 5

14

Henri Rousseau

1844–1910 ✳ FRENCH

Henri Rousseau was a gentle man with a vivid imagination. As a boy he always wanted to paint, but his family was very poor and discouraged him from even thinking of becoming an artist. He became a customs inspector instead. Nevertheless all day long as he worked at his job, he taught himself to draw by making small sketches in a notebook of the landscape around him. When he retired from inspection duties at 49, he devoted himself to art and painting. Although many people of his day did not understand his art, many leading artists, writers and critics in Paris loved his untrained, imaginative style and the fantasy quality of his paintings.

Rousseau is best known for his colorful and vivid jungle scenes. No one knows for sure where he got the ideas for these inventive jungle journeys. A popular legend is that Rousseau went to the jungles of Mexico with the French army when he was only 15. It is more likely that Rousseau never left France but transformed frequent trips to the zoo and the Paris Botanical Gardens into imaginary scenes.

Throughout his life Rousseau also loved trees, flowers and animals. Many of the species in his paintings are purely imaginary, not really existing anywhere. Because of his love and sensitivity to plant life, he became identified as the Master of the Trees by many of his fellow artists.

Rousseau's paintings have a fine decorative quality. His attention to such details as the subtle lightening of the sky, the delicate shapes of leaves, and the vivid clash of stripes on a tiger make his pictures rich in colors, patterns and shapes. Rousseau was particularly fond of the color green. He believed it was the color of life, and in some of his works he used over twenty shades. Whether or not he ever visited a jungle, Rousseau accurately captured the feeling of the tropics with his brilliant patterns of light and dark, rich and vibrant colors and animal faces partly hidden by exotic plant shapes.

Mysterious Jungles

A jungle is a place of exotic images and mysterious landscapes. Henri Rousseau used his imagination to lead people on visual journeys into fantasy jungles filled with plants and animals of his own creation.

You will need

pictures of the jungle, animals and plants
a story to read about the jungle
large butcher paper
chalk
pencils
brightly colored construction paper
scissors
glue
crayons or oil pastels

Henri Rousseau in His Office.
Photograph: The Bettmann Archive.

Tropical Storm with a Tiger (Surprised!), 1891. 51 x 63" (130 x 162 cm). The National Gallery, London

To begin

Use your imagination to create a vision of a jungle journey that you and a group of children can put together to create a jungle mural. Your imagination might lead you to see trees, flowers and plants in a way that you have not seen before. This might be the first time you become aware of some of the details in trees, animals, flowers and plants.

It is best to work in groups of four to six people for each mural. Begin by looking at different pictures of the jungle, various animals and plants. You might even want to read a story about the jungle to get your imaginations going.

Group mural, grades 1, 2 and 3.

Have one or two people from the group use chalk to block out the major areas of your picture. Include trees, plants, and animals of the jungle. The chalk will be easy to erase when you are finished with the mural.

Start working on the background. Will the sky have puffy clouds floating about? Will a fiery sun beat down on the scene below? Will there be mountains or water to define the horizon line area? What kinds of plants, flowers, and trees would you like to include? The group can work together to determine these parts of the mural. Look at the painting by Rousseau, *Tropical Storm with Tiger (Surprised!)*, and note the details of his trees, leaves, plants and flowers. Use pencils to draw your own background shapes on brightly colored construction paper. Cut them out. Glue the cut-out shapes onto the mural and use craypas or crayons to add details of texture, lines and shapes.

Think about the sights and sound in a jungle. What kinds of animals would you like for the main subjects on the mural? What will the mood in your jungle be like? What kinds of sounds will you hear? After discussing these questions, each person can pick a different animal to add to the mural. Draw the animals in pencil on construction paper and color in the details with oil pastels or crayons. When the animals are done, cut them out and glue them on the mural. Complete the work by adding color, lines and shapes where needed. When you are done, think of a story your group could tell about your mural when it is hung up. Your story might be about an adventure in the jungle.

Rudyard Kipling

1865–1936 ✳ ENGLISH

Writing was a part of Rudyard Kipling's life from the beginning. His father was a sculptor and a curator of a museum in India, where Rudyard was born. Both his parents liked to write, and his mother especially enjoyed composing verse. Many of the Kipling family's friends and relatives were artists and writers as well. Exposure to these creative people at a young age provided a rich environment in which to develop.

At a young age, Kipling was sent to a school in England, where he did a lot of reading, writing and performing in plays. He was interested in American writers and tried to imitate their style. Works by Walt Whitman, Henry Wadsworth Longfellow, Mark Twain and Edgar Allan Poe were among his favorites. He came to be respected as a writer by his classmates, who would often ask him to compose funny poems about school events.

Kipling turned his love of writing into a career. He returned to India and became a journalist, traveling widely throughout India and the world beyond in pursuit of newsworthy events. At the same time, he wrote many novels, short stories and poems about his travels.

When he and his wife were expecting a child of their own, Kipling began writing stories for children. His *Just So Stories* and *The Jungle Books* are two of his most famous. The poem "Tiger! Tiger!" can be found in *The Jungle Books*. It conjures up images of wild animals lurking in the jungle, hunting their prey.

Rudyard Kipling.
Photograph:
The Bettmann Archive.

TIGER! TIGER!

What of the hunting, hunter bold?
  Brother, the watch was long and cold.
What of the quarry ye went to kill?
  Brother, he crops in the Jungle still.
Where is the power that made
  your pride?
  Brother, it ebbs from my flank
  and side.
Where is the haste that ye hurry by?
  Brother, I go to my lair — to die!

By Rudyard Kipling

Mysterious Jungles

A jungle is a place of exotic images and mysterious landscapes. Henri Rousseau used his imagination to lead people on visual journeys into fantasy jungles filled with plants and animals of his own creation.

To begin

Pretend that you are in one of Rousseau's tropical environments. What animals do you see? Are there lions, tigers, elephants and beautiful tropical birds around? Describe what they look like. What color is the wildlife? Tell us what they are they doing. Do you see a tiger hunting, a gorilla playing or a lion at rest?

MAKING THE CONNECTION

Some artists and writers are inspired by journeys to faraway places with great adventure. Such is the case with Rousseau and Kipling, who used their experiences and imaginations to give us stories and paintings of the jungle. Rousseau's *Tropical Storm with Tiger (Surprised!)* uses the bright colors of the trees and plants and the bold colors of the animals half-hidden to convey the sense of excitement and suspense that is part of jungle life. In contrast, questions and answers in Kipling's "Tiger! Tiger!" use a more somber tone to relate the tiger to the destiny of being hunted. Both artists were able to express the feeling of a long chase, resulting in different but illuminating visions of nature in the jungle. Both take us on journeys that transport us into the imaginary world of the tiger.

Describe the plant life that surrounds you, such as trees, bushes, vines and colorful flowers. What colors do you see in the vegetation? How does it feel to be in this dangerous yet intriguing place?

Collect pictures of different environments with people or animals in them. Select one of the pictures and make a list of questions that you would ask the person or animal in it about where they live or what they are doing. Write down some of the answers they might give you.

Write a poem with a question followed by an answer, as Kipling did in "Tiger! Tiger!" You might even try to rhyme the last words of each line as he did.

The Chimpanzee

What do you do in the jungle all day?
With my friends, I laugh and play.

Where do you like to have fun?
In the trees, under the bright sun.

What do you do when the sun goes down?
I say goodnight with a sad frown.

By Ben Shapiro, grade 3

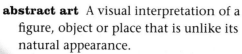

abstract art A visual interpretation of a figure, object or place that is unlike its natural appearance.

acrylic Paint containing acrylic resin that makes it dry very fast.

alliteration The repetition of initial sounds in a line or stanza.

architecture The art and science of designing and erecting buildings.

balance A state of equilibrium in which all elements are even.

ballad A song or poem that tells a story in short stanzas with simple words, often containing repetition.

batik A picture on fabric created by sealing some areas with wax and painting others with dye.

coils Spiral or ring shapes formed by rolling a piece of clay between your hands or by using fingertips to gently roll a piece of clay on a working surface.

collage A composition made by gluing paper, fabrics or any material to a background.

composition The arrangement of the parts of a work of art.

concrete poetry Poems made out of letters or words to form visual pictures, patterns or shapes.

couplet Two lines of verse that rhyme.

cylinder A tube shape formed by lines that connect and trace around the edges of two circular, parallel planar surfaces.

design The arrangement of one or more formal elements of art as an expression of the artist's concept.

edition A series of prints made from a single plate.

elements of art Color, line, shape, form, texture and balance.

environment The surroundings in which we live.

focal point The dominant point of interest that draws a viewer's eye.

folk ballad A ballad whose author is anonymous.

form The individual masses, shapes or groupings in a work of art.

found objects Any thing or things that have been gathered together to be used for something other than their original purposes.

free verse Unrhymed or loosely rhymed verse, usually with irregular stanzas, meter or rhythm. Sometimes called *blank verse*.

genre painting A realistic style of painting scenes from everyday life.

haiku A form of Japanese poetry with seventeen syllables forming three unrhymed lines, usually about nature.

hatching Lines drawn diagonally to build up an area of darkness.

horizon line The imaginary line where sky and earth meet.

illustration An example that develops or clarifies a technique or idea.

imagery Images produced in the mind by memories or use of language.

kiln An oven for firing ceramics.

landscape A depiction of natural scenery.

line An element of art used to define space, show outline or contour, or suggest volume and mass.

literary ballad A ballad for which the author is known.

lyric poem A short and very personal poem usually evoking strong emotion.

metaphor The implied comparison of two unlike objects or ideas without using *like* or *as*.

meter The measure of rhythm in verse or music.

mobile A delicately balanced sculpture that has movement and is suspended in space.

modeling A building up of three-dimensional forms in clay.

mosaic A picture formed by using small pieces of colored tile, cut-out paper or other material.

mural A long wall or ceiling painting.

narrative poetry A poem in story form.

nonobjective art Works that are expressed with the elements of art but without recognizable objects or subjects.

organic architecture Buildings that seem to flow in and out of the surrounding landscape.

papier-mâché Torn paper strips soaked in a paste solution and molded together to create a sculpture.

pastels Colored chalk.

pattern A design that repeats itself in a decorative manner.

perspective Distance represented on a two-dimensional surface.

plate A prepared surface from which prints can be made by applying pressure.

prairie house A style of long, low house with a projecting roof created by Frank Lloyd Wright, inspired by the flatness of the prairie.

printmaking The process of producing an image by applying pressure to transfer ink from an etched plate or block to paper, fabric or other material.

proportions The mathematical relationship of each part to one another and to the whole.

prose Ordinary language in written or spoken form.

quatrain Four lines of verse.

relief Sculpture in which figures project from a background.

rhyme A regular reoccurrence of sounds that are similar.

rhythm Ordered movement created by repetition of some art element.

rhythm The regular movement or flow of sounds or motions, often expressed with repetitive syllables or beats.

sculpture The creation of three-dimensional forms by carving, modeling or assembling.

shape A two-dimensional form or contour.

simile The comparison of two unlike things using *like* or *as*.

sonnet A poem containing fourteen lines, typically expressing a single theme or idea.

stabile A rigid mobile that is mounted on a platform so it stands up and is self-supporting.

stanza The division of a poem using two or more lines of verse.

symbol Something that stands for or represents another thing.

tempera An opaque, water-soluble paint.

texture The actual or implied feel of a surface.

typography The style, distribution or appearance of typed or printed matter.

ukiyo-e prints "Pictures of the floating world." Japanese prints depicting landscapes and scenes of everyday life.

value The lightness or darkness of a color.

warm colors Red, orange, yellow and brown; usually associated with fire, sun and the earth.

Babcock, Barbara, et al, *The Pueblo Storyteller: Development of a Figurative Ceramic Tradition.* Tucson, AZ: University of Arizona Press, 1986.

Bahti, Mark, *Pueblo Stories and Story Tellers.* Tucson, AZ: Treasure Chest Publications, Inc., 1988.

Barr, Alfred H., Jr. and the Museum of Modern Art, *What Is Modern Painting?* New York: The Museum of Modern Art, 1988.

Commire, Anne, ed., "Lilian Moore." *Something about the Author,* vol. 52. (Detroit: Gale Research Company, 1988): 123–131.

——— "E. B. White." *Something about the Author,* vol. 29. (Detroit: Gale Research Company, 1988): 227–238.

Davidson, Abraham A., *The Story of American Painting.* New York: Harry N. Abrams Inc.

Dittert, Alfred E., Jr., and Fred Plog, *Generations in Clay: Pueblo Pottery of the American Southwest.* Northland Publishing, 1989.

Dopagne, Jacques, *Bruegel.* New York: Leon Amiel Publishing, 1979.

Gherman, Beverly, *Georgia O'Keeffe: The "Wideness & Wonder" of Her World.* Macmillan, 1986.

——— *E. B. White, Some Writer!* New York: Atheneum, 1992.

Greiner, Donald J., ed., "Wendell Berry." *Dictionary of Literary Biography,* vol. 5. (Detroit: Gale Research Company, 1980): 63–65.

Harris, Trudier, ed. and Thadious M. Davis, assoc. ed., "Langston Hughes." *Dictionary of Literary Biography,* vol. 51. (Detroit: Gale Research Company, 1987): 112–132.

Higginson, William J., and Penny Harter, *The Haiku Handbook, How to Write, Share and Teach Haiku.* New York: McGraw-Hill Book Company, 1985.

Hopkins, Lee Bennett, *Pass the Poetry, Please!* New York: Harper Trophy, 1987.

Kaplan, Justin, *Walt Whitman, A Life.* New York: Simon and Schuster, 1980.

Lerner, Sharon, *Self-Portrait in Art.* Minneapolis, MN: Lerner Publishing Company, 1970.

Lipman, Jean, *Calder's Universe.* New York: Running Press-Whitney Museum of American Art, 1976.

Manson, Grant, *Frank Lloyd Wright to 1910: The First Golden Age.* New York: Reinhold Publishing Company, 1981.

Martin, Douglas Congdon, *Story Tellers and Other Figurative Pottery.* West Chester, PA: Schiffer Publishing Ltd.

McKissack, Patricia C., *Paul Laurence Dunbar, A Poet to Remember.* Chicago: Children's Press, 1984.

Mortimer, Hilda, with Chief Dan George, *You Call Me Chief.* New York: Doubleday and Company, Inc., 1981.

Munthe, Nelly, *Meet Matisse.* Boston, MA: Little, Brown and Company Publishing, 1983.

Myerson, Joel, ed., "Henry Wadsworth Longfellow." *Dictionary of Literary Biography,* vol. 1. (Detroit: Gale Research Company, 1978): 117–125.

——— "Walt Whitman." *Dictionary of Literary Biography,* vol. 3. (Detroit: Gale Research Company, 1979): 350–367.

Pritchard, William H., "William Carlos Williams." *Lives of the Modern Poets.* (New York: Oxford University Press, 1980): 263–294.

Quartermain, Peter, ed., "E. E. Cummings." *Dictionary of Literary Biography,* vol. 48. (Detroit: Gale Research Company, 1986): 117–137.

——— "Paul Laurence Dunbar." *Dictionary of Literary Biography,* vol. 54. (Detroit: Gale Research Company, 1987): 69–81.

Raboff, Ernest, *Henri Rousseau: Art for Children.* Harper & Row Publishers, 1988.

Rosen, Randy, et al, *Making Their Mark: Women Artists into the Mainstream.* New York: Abbeville Press Publishers, 1989.

Sills, Leslie, *Inspirations: Stories about Women Artists.* Niles, IL: Albert Whitman & Company, 1989.

Smith, Bradley, *Mexico: A History in Art.* Doubleday & Corp. Inc., 1976.

Winter, Jeanette and Jonah Winter, *Diego.* Alfred A. Knopf Publishers, Inc., 1991.

Witzling, Mara, ed., *Voicing Our Visions.* New York: Universe Publications, 1991.

Young, Robyn V., "Matsuo Bashō." Poetry Criticism, vol. 3. (Detroit: Gale Research Company, 1991): 1–33.